BonVoyage!

Travel Posters of the Edwardian Era

Julia Wigg

Published in association with
the Public Record Office

London : HMSO

© Crown copyright 1996

Applications for reproduction should be made to HMSO,
The Copyright Unit, St Clements House, 2-16 Colegate, Norwich NR3 1BQ

ISBN 0 11 440261 2

The author has asserted her right to be identified as the author of this work
British Library Cataloguing in Publication Data
A CIP catalogue record for this book is available from the British Library
Designed, edited and produced by HMSO

Published by HMSO and available from:

HMSO Publications Centre
(Mail, fax and telephone orders only)
PO Box 276, London SW8 5DT
Telephone orders 0171 873 9090
General enquiries 0171 873 0011
(queuing system in operation for both numbers)
Fax orders 0171 873 8200

HMSO Bookshops
49 High Holborn, London WC1V 6HB
(counter service only)
0171 873 0011 Fax 0171 831 1326
68–69 Bull Street, Birmingham B4 6AD
0121 236 9696   Fax 0121 236 9699
33 Wine Street, Bristol BS1 2BQ
0117 9264306 Fax 0117 9294515
9–21 Princess Street, Manchester M60 8AS
0161 834 7201 Fax 0161 833 0634
16 Arthur Street, Belfast BT1 4GD
01232 238451 Fax 01232 235401
71 Lothian Road, Edinburgh EH3 9AZ
0131 228 4181 Fax 0131 229 2734
The HMSO Oriel Bookshop
The Friary, Cardiff CF1 4AA
01222 395548 Fax 01222 384347

HMSO's Accredited Agents
(see Yellow Pages)

and through good booksellers

Printed in the United Kingdom for HMSO
Dd 302384 C60 6/96

Contents

ACKNOWLEDGEMENTS

I should like to express my thanks to colleagues at the Public Record Office for their help. In particular I am most grateful to Jo Matthews, who first pointed me in the direction of the posters, and to Jim Murray whose enthusiasm and advice sustained me whenever I needed encouragement. A special word of thanks goes also to my husband Chris and our sons Patrick and David for their support at home while I was writing the book. The photographs of the posters were taken by Andrew Smart of AC Cooper Ltd, Brian Carter of the PRO and Miki Slingsby.

Posters and Publicity

Travel posters from the early years of the twentieth century offer us a glimpse of an era when the idea of travel for pleasure had begun to take root, not merely in the wealthier sections of Edwardian society, but among the poorer classes too. They can tell us where people went, whether it was for seaside holidays, short day trips into London or the countryside, or extended excursions abroad, and how they travelled there. They give us an indication of how the railway and shipping companies regarded the travelling public; and we can see how these perceptions were reflected in the different levels at which the companies pitched their advertising and the various themes they used within it.

The posters that form this book are part of the extensive archive of Victorian and Edwardian advertising material held in the Public Record Office at Kew. They are attached to the original application forms that were used to register design copyright at Stationers' Hall under Acts of Parliament in force from 1842 to 1912. As it was not compulsory to register copyright and many firms obviously did not feel it was worth the trouble and expense (a penny for a form, a shilling to register and five shillings for a certificate), this inevitably means that we do not have a complete picture of Edwardian travel advertising – some companies, particularly the smaller railway lines, are not represented in the archive at all. But enough did so to give us a flavour of the destinations and travel arrangements by land and sea that were on offer to the prospective traveller at the time. Strictly speaking, the Edwardian period runs from January 1901 to May 1910, but the Stationers' Hall archive extends to April 1912. It seems unnecessarily pedantic to exclude material from the last two years, particularly as some of the most interesting Tube advertising dates from 1911, and there was certainly no sudden change in artistic style to coincide with the death of the king. 'Edwardian' bears a slightly more elastic interpretation than usual, but it is still the most convenient label to use for the whole of the period covered in this book.

A slice of social history comes alive in these posters: they tell us very clearly how the railway and shipping companies tried to attract potential passengers. All advertisements are designed to arouse a response in us: they have to be sufficiently attractive, amusing or otherwise interesting to stimulate us into action – in this case, into buying a railway or boat ticket. This is where sober fact is glossed over and the world of fantasy begins – the world of relaxed holidays, speedy, efficient journeys and sumptuous accommodation. Even in the Edwardian era of ostentation and conspicuous consumption, at least by the upper classes, this was not always the case! Reality was more mundane.

These posters are also interesting in terms of graphic design. The earlier ones are mostly very busy, often cluttered with type laid over composite views (see left, and plates 11 and 26). Later on simpler, more arresting images come to the fore, particularly those of the more progressive companies such as the Great Northern Railway or the Midland Railway (see right, and plates 14 and 36). The influence of late nineteenth-century French poster artists such as Jules Cheret, Toulouse-Lautrec or the Czech painter Alphonse Mucha slowly trickled across the Channel and was absorbed into British notions of design via the more experimental artists such as Aubrey Beardsley, the Beggarstaffs and Dudley Hardy. In France at this

Non-stop long-distance travel on the Great Western Railway was excellent by 1904: dining cars and corridor trains with lavatories assured the comfort of passengers and the service was fast and reliable. COPY 1/218 folio 255

Shipping companies were in the forefront of effective travel advertising in the Edwardian period; here the vast bulk of a Cunard liner is seen from a very low viewpoint looming over the waves. COPY 1/315i folio 137

time the poster was accepted as a serious art form and was regarded as an integral part of an artist's output. But in Britain, fine artists tended on the whole to regard a poster commission as merely bread-and-butter work, not usually worthy of serious attention. The world of entertainment, particularly the theatre, did attract some of the better poster designers but travel advertising, shackled to some degree by innately conservative members of company boards, at first lagged behind.

The advent of colour lithography and its increasing use from the 1870s revolutionised advertising design. Before that posters were mainly typographical in form with the occasional wood engraving. Now it was possible to have text and images wholly integrated but designers took some time to make full use of the possibilities for travel posters. At first they still tended to rely on rather uninteresting views of the landscape topped and tailed with type, but later more original images were produced with sometimes just the name of the company in large letters (see plates 8 and 46).

Towards the end of the nineteenth century the quantity of advertising material on display was enormous. A great deal of it was on station hoardings and buildings so it made sense for the railway companies themselves to use their own sites for their own advertising. By the turn of the century most of the dozens of railway companies had a publicity department, however small, although much of the work was contracted out to printers (or later on to advertising agencies) with virtually no direct contact between the company and the artist. The style and standard of posters were therefore very variable. Some artists did work mainly for specific companies (Alec Fraser for the Great Western Railway, for example, or John Hassall for the Great Northern) but properly co-ordinated campaigns did not really begin until the start of centralised Underground advertising towards the end of the Edwardian era.

The Travel, Sports and Pastimes Exhibition held at Olympia in 1909 drew large crowds and whetted the appetite of the public for foreign travel by rail and steamship. Big-game hunting in Africa and India was a particular attraction. COPY 1/281 folio 36

Travel abroad became more common around the turn of the century as the country prospered and foreign trips came within the means of a wider cross-section of society. Shipping companies, travel agents and railways abroad, especially in the British Empire, all advertised more widely to gain a share of the growing market. Interest was stimulated too by large exhibitions such as the Empire of India Exhibition of 1895, the Franco-British Exhibition of 1908 (see plate 52) or the Travel, Sports and Pastimes Exhibition of 1909, all of which informed the public of destinations further afield.

Relatively long-distance travel for pleasure, both abroad and within Britain, became much more viable as the trains and ships themselves became more comfortable. Sleeping-cars were introduced in Britain in 1873, though to begin with only for first-class accommodation, and the Great Western Railway persisted in denying sleep to third-class passegers until 1928. Originally each carriage was self-contained with no means of access to the next, but gradually corridor trains came into use, which meant that passengers in all compartments had access to a lavatory. 'Corridor trains' is a line that very often appears on posters – they were clearly regarded as being a very important element of any railway's efforts to make life easy for passengers. Before this frequent stops were necessary on long journeys!

Dining-cars were another big improvement. The Great Northern Railway was the first to provide a dining-car service for its first-class passengers in 1879, and this idea spread rapidly to other companies. Railway advertising stressed these additional

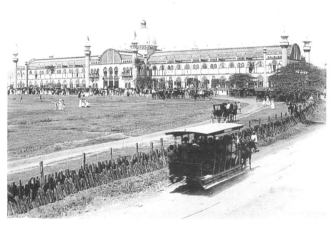

Exhibition mania extended to the colonies – this is the magnificent exhibition building in Kingston, Jamaica, seen at the turn of the century. COPY 1/400

features whenever they were available as comfort on the journey was seen as an effective promotional tool. The Great Western Railway in particular concentrated on this aspect: nearly all their posters for longer journeys mention corridor trains and dining-cars. Speed and punctuality were also emphasised in advertisements as essential elements of an efficient service. Arrangements for luggage were frequently mentioned too. People travelled with a huge range of different types and sizes: vast unwieldy leather trunks which resembled chests of drawers when the outer cover was removed; haversacks; dressing-cases; hatboxes; boxes for stiff collars, detachable cuffs, sets of brushes and other necessities. 'Luggage conveyed free' was a point to be considered when you had so much impedimenta, especially if you had to change trains or embark on a steamer with it all.

No expense was spared here in this splendid dining saloon car, used on the Great Eastern Railway's east coast service in the Edwardian period. Thickly upholstered dining chairs and polished wood panelling contribute to its air of solid comfort.
COPY 1/432 folio 13

The Edwardian traveller found it impossible to move without a vast assortment of trunks and boxes, particularly when travelling by sea. Railway companies knew this – in 1904 the Great Northern Railway allowed third-class passengers to have 60 lb of luggage conveyed free, and first-class up to 120 lb! COPY 1/178 folio 140

Shipping companies paid just as much attention as railways did to making the surroundings as pleasant as possible for their passengers and using this to the full in their publicity material. Well-appointed cabins, spacious public areas and a comfortable, stable crossing were paramount, especially in advertising for transatlantic and cruise liners, whose first-class sections were comparable with the very smartest hotels. Ships generally still had three classes of accommodation, but even the second class was very good, 'like first class on a small scale', according to Arnold Bennett *en route* for the United States in 1911. 'Less space. Had we not been in first class it would have seemed spacious and magnificent. Little difference in berths.' Agreeable surroundings and reliable service on the voyage or train journey gave rise to the idea of regarding the time spent travelling as an intrinsic part of the holiday and both rail and shipping companies constructed much of their poster advertising around this notion.

Beside the Sea

PLATES 1–11

The habit of taking a holiday by the sea began to flourish in the late eighteenth century as a descendant of the earlier vogue for spending time at an inland watering-place or spa, initially for health reasons, later for leisure and entertainment of other sorts. In time bathing in sea-water came to be regarded as being a healthy pursuit too. Seaside towns began to displace the inland centres in popularity, but spas such as Bath and Droitwich continued to be promoted as good places for getting rid of ills. Scarborough was one of the few towns that were both traditional watering-place and newly popular sea-bathing resort, though one had to be particularly hardy to brave the rigours of the North Sea. All the east coast resorts made the most of their windy weather, emphasising their claims to a climate perfect for health and fitness, just the place to blow away your cares. The railway companies serving this area built on and expanded this reputation: one of the most famous posters ever produced was John Hassall's 1908 design for the Great Northern Railway 'Skegness is So Bracing' and he produced another winner for the same company three years later (see plate 8).

3

Resorts in the south and south-west angled their material rather differently: they were promoted more for their picturesque scenery and aimed at more sedate travellers. The beauties of nature and the supposed mildness of climate are common elements of advertisements for these areas, particularly in Dorset and Devon.

The majority of holiday resort posters were an integral part of the railway companies' own advertising for their train services, but a number were produced in conjunction with local town councils. There are even a few examples published by councils alone or by local advertising associations (see the poster for Southsea and Portsmouth, plate 3). This input by local worthies undoubtedly led sometimes to rather conservative designs: standard landscape views, frilly borders, too much type – all of which were elements of late Victorian taste. Many are attractive to us now as slightly nostalgic bygone images but it is difficult to gauge how successful they were as eye-catching advertisements at the time of publication. Seen at a distance, fussy pictorial details would become meaningless and any text set in small type would have melted into illegibility. A writer in the *Railway and Travel Monthly* for March 1913 acknowledged this: 'No one would ever dream of spending time in reading them, and it is gratifying to see that the tendency today is to abolish this kind of poster, and to issue ones on which pictures alone suffice, there being scarcely any printing matter other than the name of the railway concerned.'

During the first few years of the Edwardian era travel advertisements gradually abandoned the old-fashioned style. Bolder designs were produced which relied on one good strong image, however general, to give a holiday atmosphere. One example is the Broadstairs poster with children happily playing on the sand under the cliffs (plate 22): another is the London and South Western Railway poster for Weymouth, showing a girl feeding swans (plate 7). This does not immediately conjure up a vision of the seaside but is undoubtedly a forceful and uncluttered design. The triumph of image over information appears *par excellence* in the Great Western Railway August Bank Holiday poster for 1903 (plate 12).

A theme common to the advertising of seaside towns as train travel destinations is that of the family (idealised in plate 13). The companies predicted that there would be

a lucrative bucket-and-spade market waiting to be tapped and a large number of holiday resort posters use images of children (see, for example, the Great Northern Railway poster of children paddling, plate 9, or the Swanage poster, plate 10). The idea that if your children are happy you are more likely to have a relatively stress-free holiday is not a new one. Some posters did not rely on the image alone but reinforced it with a suitable slogan: Broadstairs (plate 22) was promoted as 'the children's Elysium' and the child in the Swanage poster is saying 'I feel so jolly here'. As the yoke of poverty lightened, more families began to have

The beach at Shanklin, Isle of Wight, about 1905. Then as now its wide sands and safe bathing made it a resort especially popular with families. RAIL 411/538

enough money left over after the basic necessities to afford some time away from home but it was still mainly the upper and middle classes who could afford a family holiday of a week or fortnight, rather than the occasional day trip.

By the late nineteenth century the railway network in Britain was very extensive and almost every small town had access to it. The first railways were built in response to a demand for the carriage of freight but almost from the beginning the passenger element was important as a source of revenue. By the middle of the nineteenth century lower ticket prices had greatly increased demand. Originally there were three classes of carriage, though not all companies ran third-class carriages on all trains. It was a legal requirement to provide for all destinations at least one service per day on which passengers could travel in third class at a cost of a penny a mile (known as Parliamentary fares). In 1872 the Midland Railway, always an innovative company, decided that third-class passengers would be conveyed on all trains at Parliamentary fares. This immediately resulted in a large increase in third-class passengers and caused other companies at once to reduce their third-class fares too to remain in the market. Three years later the Midland introduced another radical change: they abolished second class entirely and reduced first-class fares. This time not all their competitors did the same. The London and North Western Railway kept second class until 1911, and Sir George Findlay, its general manager, wrote that the company 'maintained the belief that society in this country, for all purposes, naturally divided itself into three classes.' Servants travelling with their employers normally went second class, where there was still such a division, sometimes at reduced fares (see the Great Western Railway poster for the hunting season, plate 21). Some services particularly emphasised the first-class element, such as the *Southern Belle* (plate 16). Others concentrated on the other end of the market, such as many of the third-class seaside excursions to favourite working-class resorts.

The railway companies and holiday resorts depended very closely on each other for mutual growth. Commercial concerns in seaside towns realised that a railway link was absolutely essential if a resort was to be developed successfully. Most large resorts began by catering primarily for the wealthy and middle classes, then later extended their range of accommodation and amusements to provide for the needs of the working classes as well. Therefore both large smart hotels and cheap boarding houses were built, although the fashionable and expensive area in any town was usually slightly removed from the cheap and cheerful. If the town boasted cliffs overlooking a fine bay the good hotels would be there, deliberately set far from the madding crowd below. What were once small fashionable resorts now opened up to the masses, though a few smaller places such as Tenby and Lyme Regis tried to remain select and deliberately avoided making any provision for cheap lodgings or popular entertainment, particularly if the town was a long distance from London or other centres. Some larger resorts, Bournemouth and Torquay for instance, also continued to aim firmly for wealthy holidaymakers and to ignore the working classes as far as possible.

Marine Parade East, Lyme Regis. Mixed bathing was permitted by most town councils in England in the Edwardian period, but respectability was ensured by means of the bathing machines still in regular use here. RAIL 411/538

Large capital sums were invested in seaside towns, and not just by the railway companies. There was much private investment too in hotels, shops and places of entertainment, and also public investment in piers, municipal parks, bandstands, wide promenades and other amenities. Bathing machines were still in existence in several places at the turn of the century (see the poster for Swanage, plate 10) but their use was becoming less widespread and beach tents reminiscent of those on medieval battlefields were becoming the norm instead.

It is a strange fact that in the Edwardian era virtually no holiday resort sold itself by means of sexual titillation, however delicately hinted at: no conventional bathing belles appeared on posters, although scantily clad female figures were used regularly to advertise all sorts of other products such as lighting, bicycles, drinks, luggage and so on.

Only a few posters even used images of couples, perhaps sitting on a convenient bench or walking along the esplanade (see the poster for Great Yarmouth, plate 5). The railway companies were clearly very keen to be seen as entirely respectable: the whole thrust of their advertising for rail travel to the seaside was aimed squarely at the family and concentrated on the benefits of a healthy break outdoors in the breezy English climate.

A common sight on beaches a hundred years ago was the bathing machine, a sort of rudimentary beach hut on wheels in which you changed for your dip. It was then trundled by horse power into several feet of water so that you could jump straight in, avoiding prying eyes. Some even had awnings to let down over the door for extra modesty.
COPY 1/91 folios 131 and 132

Away Days

PLATES 12–24

The origins of railway excursions and cheap return trips lie at the very beginning of railway history. In 1841 Thomas Cook, then a printer and itinerant preacher and Bible reader, had the idea that made his fortune. For one of his temperance meetings he secured a special train from Leicester to Loughborough: this carried passengers for a shilling each, and with it the cheap excursion traffic may be said to have begun. Other trips were arranged by Cook, who soon had a regular arrangement with the Midland Railway. Their association continued for decades (see, for example, the posters for travel to Ireland and London, plates 36, 50 and 51). It proved extremely successful and the idea was taken up by other entrepreneurs almost immediately. Rowland Hill, of penny post fame, organised the first seaside one in 1843 on the Brighton line. Conditions were very basic to start with and improvements in services took a long time to reach all classes of passengers. Excursions were not always welcomed by regular travellers: an aggrieved passenger wrote in the *Railway Herald Magazine* of March 1896 that on Sundays and Bank Holidays there were trains a plenty for those who 'wanted to travel in droves from big centres to certain points' but far fewer trains than usual for anywhere even faintly out of the way: 'Excursion trains, although a great boon to the humbler classes and the economically inclined, are not best calculated for the ordinary traveller.'

Early posters advertising excursions included a mass of practical information and were similar to the old railway handbills. These were usually lists set in a muddle of different styles and weights of typeface, with an occasional engraving at the top or in the centre. When large pictorial posters began to be used, the amount of lettering had to be reduced as too much type could detract from the forcefulness of the image (see the posters for the *Southern Belle* or the Marlborough and Calne service, plates 16 and 20). The way round the problem was usually to produce a striking general poster (see plates 12, 15 and 18), with the company's name or the destination prominently displayed, saying that full particulars were available on application to the station.

Trips were laid on at the weekend and often on Mondays too (not just on Bank Holiday Mondays). This was probably a hangover from the old habit of the 'St Monday' holiday when workers frequently took an unauthorised day off to recover from the excesses of the weekend. By 1900 the number of day trips arranged, especially during the spring and summer, had risen enormously, with a vast exodus at weekends from London to the coast or country beauty spots. The Great Northern Railway, for instance, regularly ran summer day trips from King's Cross to the east coast resorts such as Skegness or Mablethorpe by non-stop corridor train for three shillings, a remarkable bargain. The South Eastern and Chatham Railway ran daily circular tours during the summer, with its trippers setting off from Folkestone by steamer via Dover, Deal and Ramsgate to Margate and returning by rail from Margate to Folkestone.

Christmas was also a time for excursions (see the Great Northern Railway and Great Western Railway posters, plates 14 and 15) as almost everyone had at least a day or two off then. As more workers began to have paid holidays, the scope for day trips increased in terms of both time and affordability. The poorer classes who were unable to afford a family seaside holiday for a week or fortnight could still sometimes manage occasional cheap excursions, if they were able to go somewhere not too far from home. Londoners, for instance, patronised the north Kent and Essex resorts (see the posters for Broadstairs and Southend, plates 22 and 23), and urban dwellers from Birmingham and Manchester made trips into the Peak District, or to the North Wales and Lancashire coasts.

An excursion could be almost anything from a cheap day out for townsfolk into the nearest patch of accessible countryside, to an expensive and exclusive return trip on a train such as the *Southern Belle* (see plate 16). Inaugurated in 1908, this was the special first-class-only Pullman service to Brighton run by the London, Brighton and South Coast Railway. It was advertised as 'the most luxurious train in the world', and with good reason. It consisted of a dining-car and six drawing-room cars, each decorated in an individual but always very elaborate style. Much use was made of different types of panelling, inlaid woods, ornately framed large mirrors, fine ironwork and so on. The table tops were of rich curl veneer and on them were placed 'standard lamps of exquisite form, beautifully chased and gilded', according to a report in the *Railway and Travel Monthly* of October 1910. It went on to describe further wonders: 'The ladies' and gentlemen's toilets are furnished with all the latest improvements. The washstands are finished with onyx marble tops and the woodwork is of a fine stripe mahogany.' Brighton was regarded as the ideal place for excursions from the metropolis and its nickname in Edwardian days was London-on-Sea. The town catered for the lower orders as well as wealthy travellers arriving on the *Southern Belle*: there were plenty of cheap boarding houses and rooms to let in the less smart parts of town away from the seafront. The cheap day return fare, available on Sundays and Mondays, was three shillings, and on Bank Holidays it increased to four. The fare on the *Southern Belle* was twelve shillings.

A crowd of holidaymakers, well wrapped up against chilly breezes, pile into the carriages of Southend pier's electric railway in June 1891. It conveyed passengers the mile out to sea and was very popular with day-trippers. COPY 1/404

Trips into the countryside were also very popular. The Great Western Railway tended to be best known for its long-distance lines to the West Country and South Wales but the company also made efforts to promote stations nearer to London as excellent starting points for days in the country. It produced a series of posters advertising trips to places west of London such as Beaconsfield, Burnham Beeches, Windsor and Eton and various points in the Thames Valley. The Brighton Railway also cashed in on the fact that its route to the coast lay across the Sussex Downs and promoted the area in its own right for day or weekend trips (see plate 18).

The pursuit of pleasure as more people had more leisure time available was a concept eagerly embraced by the railway companies. The Glasgow and South Western Railway, for instance, frequently used the slogan 'the Golfers' Line' and prominently advertised its stations as being convenient for many of the golf courses of south-west Scotland. The Lancashire and Yorkshire Railway promoted the Ribble Valley as 'the Ideal Picnic District' and ran special picnic trains on Saturdays between June and September. And many of the railway companies issued their own maps and guide books aimed at the holidaymaker and excursionist.

The Furness Railway (see plate 19) is a particularly good example of how railway companies in the Edwardian age attempted to attract new passengers with a variety of special excursions. Of course in one sense their job was made easier by the fact that this was well before the days of widespread motoring so they were not in competition with the private car. The Furness line, originally built to serve the mineral-mining towns of the Cumberland coast, skirted the Lake District along its southern and western edges and wherever practicable made a dart into the interior. The company operated steamers on Windermere and Lake Coniston and motor-coaches to fill in any gaps that were only possible to cover by road. Several circular tours were advertised: one was from Barrow by train to Lake Side (on Windermere), by steamer to the head of Lake Windermere, coach to Coniston and thence by train back to Barrow. First- and third-class carriages were provided. The tours were widely advertised and the Furness Railway arranged travel to Barrow from the industrial cities of the north-west in conjunction with the Midland Railway and the London and North Western Railway: trains from Liverpool, Manchester, Leeds, Bradford and other towns connected with the Furness line at Carnforth. The company's prime object was of course to make a handsome profit for its shareholders, but a subsidiary one was to do this through a mixture of business acumen and philanthropy. Its third-class excursion fares were deliberately set as low as possible to appeal to the working classes. 'No respectable artisan, with limited holiday opportunities and limited purse, need be deterred by either consideration from enjoying the most beautiful sights and scenery in the country. What this means to a Lancashire mill hand, whose occupation from day to day is sordid and depressing, and who can now so easily breathe the inspiration due to a communion with Nature at her grandest, can scarcely be estimated,' wrote a contributor to the *Railway and Travel Monthly* of August 1910.

The Celtic Fringe
PLATES 25–37

By the beginning of the twentieth century Britain's rail network covered the land: travel to the furthest corners was becoming commonplace and was reflected in the large numbers of travel posters promoting the Celtic lands of Cornwall, Wales, Scotland and Ireland. They were meant to appeal to a slightly different market: instead of the heavy emphasis on family life that is apparent in most of the posters advertising resorts on the east and south coasts, scenery is the mainstay. Beaches, bandstands, piers and promenades were out; cliffs, gorges, rivers, lochs and mountains were in. The dramatic cliff walks and coastal scenery of Wales and Cornwall often appear in the posters, as do bens and glens in the advertisements for Scotland. Literary associations figure largely too, especially in the Scottish material: quotations from Burns or Scott are quite common and the Glasgow and South Western Railway promoted its area as the 'Land o' Burns'.

There were exceptions to the rule. The Great Western Railway's publicity department was content to use a fairly standard style of design whatever the resort. They produced a number of advertisements for Cornwall and South Wales which were in essence very similar to their posters for towns in other areas such as Somerset and Dorset and very often by the same artists. Alec Fraser was one they used frequently and his style is very distinctive, particularly in his use of fat, solid lettering, in which he may have been inspired by contemporary French art. His posters for Weymouth, Tenby and New Quay in South Wales (plates 2, 29 and 30) are all full of it. The soft greens, blues and oranges make all these resorts look similarly warm, sunny and inviting. The Weymouth and New Quay ones are especially alike and clearly examples of formulaic hack-work, but they are nevertheless attractive, possibly more to us now than to contemporary viewers, as we see them through rose-coloured spectacles tinted by nostalgia for times past.

The London and North Western Railway was particularly keen to promote the coast of North Wales, served by its route to Holyhead in Anglesey. Much of its advertising used the slogan 'the Business and Pleasure Line'. Towns such as Colwyn Bay and Llandudno were portrayed as winter health resorts and some of the claims made for them were rather fanciful: 'the dry, mild and equable climate peculiarly adapts this District for the relief of pulmonary and other disorders'. A list of the town's attractions included steam-heated trains to get you there, 'invalid carriages', mountain and sea air and the fact that the resort was 'free from fogs'. The Edwardians made serious efforts to enjoy their hypochondria to the full and the London and North Western Railway undoubtedly pandered to this foible, seizing the opportunity to increase revenue.

A few advertisements for the more far-flung corners of Britain used the image of the railway engine itself (see the poster for travel by the Midland Railway to Scotland, plate 31). We now think of the steam train as part of the romance of bygone travel, but to the Edwardians it was simply the normal mode of transport and therefore not regarded as particularly worthy of remark except when some new element was introduced such as a dining-car or a non-stop service. The Great Western Railway in particular ran a series of non-stop long-distance trains in the summer months. The longest of these, the *Cornish Riviera Ltd* express service from Paddington to Plymouth, covered the 246 miles in 265 minutes and was promoted as the longest non-stop journey in Europe.

Some Scottish travel companies continued to use very traditional themes in their advertising, depicting stags glimpsed through the mist, heather-clad hillsides, steamers on the lochs and baronial halls on the shore. Scotland had been popular as an upmarket holiday destination ever since Queen Victoria bought Balmoral Castle and spent increasingly long periods of time there. As Anthony Trollope ironically remarked in *The Eustace Diamonds*: 'You will meet an earl or at least a lord on every mountain. Of course, if you merely travel about from inn to inn, and neither have a moor of your own nor stay with any great friend, you don't quite enjoy the cream of it; but to go to Scotland in August, and stay there, perhaps, till the end of September, is about the most certain step you can take towards autumnal fashion'. Association with royalty, however tenuous, was regarded as a legitimate and indeed useful little extra for the sales pitch. 'Royal route' summer tours, for example, in the Western Highlands and islands of Scotland were run by the Royal Mail steamers of David MacBrayne Ltd (see plate 33).

At this time Ireland was entirely under the British Crown and was clearly a favoured destination for travellers. It was well supplied with steamer services by various routes (see the poster advertising the direct route to Ireland, plate 34). The London and North Western Railway owned and operated a steamer service from Holyhead to Dublin which connected with trains on both sides of the Irish Sea, enabling them to boast of providing travel between London and Dublin in 13 hours.

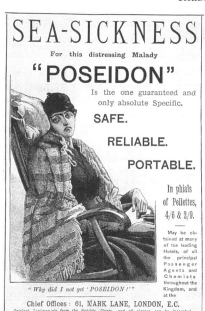

Increasing numbers of passengers sailing across the English Channel, the Irish Sea and even the North Atlantic meant more business for the makers of remedies for the perennial problem of seasickness. COPY 1/109 folio 2

There was always hot competition for the lucrative passenger traffic. In 1904, for example, the Midland Railway began to run a ferry service to Ireland from Heysham, where they had just completed the construction of a large harbour. Immediately the London and North Western Railway responded by speeding up its London to Belfast service via Holyhead and Greenore. The Great Western Railway was not to be outdone – they concentrated on southern Ireland, running a service to Rosslare from Fishguard in South Wales. Posters for ferries and liners frequently used the image of the boat itself, sailing into the sunset or towering over the quayside (see plates 34 and 47). The aim was to impress potential passengers with the magnificence of the vessel and to reassure them, through its solidity and size, of its innate safety and stability. Nothing could prevent ships from rolling in rough seas, however: seasickness remedies were as popular then as always.

Ireland was promoted as a place for perfect rest and relaxation, with advertisements concentrating on the beauties of the soft green landscape, especially in the southern counties. Many of the posters consist of attractive views of the local scenery, fairly realistic in style, with hardly a human figure to be seen. Advertisers played on the traditional symbols of Ireland (see, for example, the shamrock shape of the Larne travel agent's poster, plate 37). One or two more unusual images have survived, such as the very striking Midland Railway poster in navy and yellow (plate 36) which depicts the cliffs at Carrick-a-Rede and the rope bridge slung across the gaping chasm between them.

Foreign Fields

PLATES 38–49

Even though the habit of taking holidays abroad, which had become fairly widespread among those who could afford it by the Edwardian era, was partly due to the greater ease of travelling, the ideas behind it go back to the eighteenth century. The 'Grand Tour' round Europe and perhaps the Near East, undertaken by scions of wealthy families to complete their education, was the forerunner of foreign holidays, rather as weeks at the seaside arose from the tradition of taking the waters. By the end of the nineteenth century, travel overseas was perceived much less as a means of self-improvement, and more as a form of pleasure for its own sake, which might perhaps as an added bonus broaden the traveller's mind along the way, and the concept of free time as something to be enjoyed rather than filled was by then a widespread notion.

Travel to the continent was heavily promoted. The London, Brighton and South Coast Railway ran trips to various European capitals such as Paris and Vienna via their steamer service from Newhaven to Dieppe. They also produced 'a dainty little illustrated booklet entitled *The Riviera and Italy for a £10 Note*, giving particulars of an enchanting tour, embracing the whole of the beautiful coast from Cette to Genoa inclusive', according to the *Railway Magazine* for 1900. As more seaside towns in Britain became full of the poorer classes, those who considered themselves socially superior retreated to Europe, either to the French and Belgian side of the Channel if they simply wanted a rather more exclusive holiday by the sea, or to the smart resorts of Switzerland or Italy for mountain air and sightseeing.

Railway companies abroad advertised their services in Britain too, particularly French lines. A contributor to the *Railway Magazine* of 1901 sampled the fast and efficient services of the Chemin de Fer du Nord to Paris and wryly commented: 'Such splendid performances of the Nord only tend to throw into greater shade the mediocre connecting services of the South-East and Chatham railway'. *Plus ça change, plus c'est la même chose.* In return, British railway companies, several of which operated steamer services to the continent, tried to attract foreign tourists. The London and South Western Railway published a bilingual guide-book to the holiday resorts it served on the south coast, and a few French-language posters were produced to promote English services (see the Great Western Railway Brest à Londres poster, plate 39).

By late Victorian times most of the railway network was in place across Europe, North America and to a lesser extent Africa and Asia. All over the British Empire companies realised the value of publicity in the mother country as the numbers of relatively wealthy travelling public increased and looked outside Britain and Western Europe for their leisure travel. Egypt had long been a favoured destination for exotic holidays by the more adventurous type of traveller, and P&O ran a regular service there as well as including it on some of their cruises (see plate 40). Other African countries deeper into the continent began to open up too, such as Rhodesia and Sudan, promoted as being the ideal country for 'Health and Sport'. The Sudan Government Railway maintained a Chief European Passenger Agent with offices in London and 'the booklets and posters prepared by him have already taken their place in the front rank of railway publicity', according to the *Railway and Travel Monthly* of January 1913. On the whole, African railway advertising concentrated heavily on big game shooting, as seen in the posters for the Uganda Railway (plates 42 and 43). By contrast, travel in India was rather more sophisticated than in Africa: a complicated railway network had grown up under the British Raj and by 1900 extended all over the sub-continent. One of the companies was the Great Indian Peninsula Railway, whose publicity department concentrated on advertising their services to the wealthy colonials who aimed to make their stay in India a rather more gracious version of living in England. The company's trains were promoted as the last word in comfort, comparable with anything back home (see, for example, the poster for travel to Poona Races, plate 41).

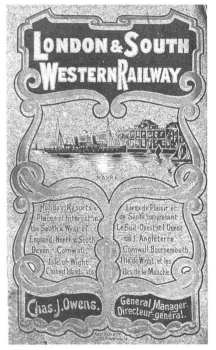

The London and South Western Railway were alive to the possibility of French people travelling to Britain for their holidays. In 1905 they produced a useful bilingual guide to the south coast resorts served by their lines. RAIL 411/538

Travel across the Atlantic was not entirely for business purposes or because of emigration. There was a small but steadily growing number of people with enough time and money to contemplate holidays in the United States, Canada or even one or two of the Caribbean islands such as Jamaica. Some notable posters were put out at this time by transatlantic services: Cunard's eye-catching globe (plate 46) and its advertisement featuring the *Lusitania* (plate 47) are both very attractive, as is the Dominion Line's poster for travel to Canada (plate 45) showing passengers promenading on the deck. The shipping lines which held a government contract to carry the Royal Mail never lost an opportunity to use this as part of their advertising: it was regarded in a similar light to the royal seal of approval, 'by appointment to Her Majesty the Queen', in terms of implying reliability and respectability (see the Imperial Direct West India Mail and the Cunard *Lusitania* posters, plates 44 and 47).

Edwardian tourists did not have to make their own travel arrangements independently, unless they wanted to: package tours began in 1861, when on 15 May the first Cook's tour set out for Paris, and were very well established by 1900. Cook's (plate 38) was the largest firm and there were a host of others such as Lunn's, Frames, Pickfords (plate 48), the Co-operative Holiday Association, and smaller concerns like A1 Tours (plate 49). Travel abroad for pleasure was strongly supported by all the passenger shipping lines, whether operating cross-Channel ferries or transatlantic liners. Several had by this period diversified into cruises in addition to their scheduled services. In May 1910, for example, P&O was advertising pleasure cruises of two or three weeks to the Azores in spring, the Norwegian fjords and the Baltic in summer, and Dalmatia, Venice, Greece and Constantinople in the autumn. The desire for foreign travel seems to be a particularly Anglo-Saxon trait – perhaps we all want to escape our cool and cloudy skies once in a while. As the boat train for Dover swept through Dulwich station in October 1897, Arnold Bennett caught a glimpse from his carriage window of a few souls waiting for an ordinary service to town and noted in his journal: 'It was impossible not to feel uplifted by a feeling of superiority. In the minds of how many on that platform is not the continental train, as it thunders past every morning, the visible symbol of pleasure, adventure and romance!'

Up to Town
PLATES 50–60

Railway companies were very keen to encourage the travelling public to make trips to London. Some of the most immediately striking posters of this period were a large series produced by Thomas Cook in conjunction with the Midland Railway to promote travel to the capital (see the posters of the Chelsea pensioner and Piccadilly, plates 50 and 51). Many of these are simple two - or three-colour images with high contrast, making use of well-known landmarks but managing to do so in a fresh and attractive way. Some had only the basic image printed and were used almost as stock posters: blank space was left in the design so that detailed information could be over-printed later, particularly when special excursions were being promoted.

The Midland Railway series concentrated on London for sightseeing and cultural experience. In contrast, advertising material produced by the London underground and suburban lines was firmly based on the joys of London as a centre for good shops and theatres or other entertainment (see the Central London Railway shopping poster and the Underground to the theatre poster, plates 53 and 54). An air of smartness and elegance was an important element of much London travel advertising and many of the posters included figures immaculately attired from top to toe, such as the stylish young woman in yellow who dominates the shopping poster (plate 53).

As the London underground lines were built by several different railway companies, they naturally began by advertising their services separately (see, for example, the Central London Railway poster for travel to the Franco-British Exhibition, plate 52). A simple map or diagram of the route was often included on the posters (see plates 52 and 59), sometimes with an indication of the stations where there was an interchange with other lines, but posters showing complete maps of the system were rare.

On 1 January 1911 interchangeable ticketing came into force throughout the underground railways. Co-ordinated advertising was the obvious next step: the familiar Underground lettering in small capitals with the U and D in large capitals at each end of the word began to appear then on Underground posters (see plates 54, 57 and 58). It was a successful and well-liked style that was to continue unchanged for decades.

Those sections of the Underground which served the outer margins of the capital were keen to increase passenger traffic at the weekends. They embarked on a campaign to promote inexpensive trips into the country, aimed particularly at encouraging the working classes to regard the Tube as a means of access to good healthy outdoor pursuits. A contributor to the *Railway and Travel Monthly* of June 1913 commented approvingly: 'What the effect of the revolution in short distance travelling facilities has meant to the poorer classes it is hard to say without being accused of exaggerating. After a week spent in the heart of the city – not merely the hours of business, but an uninterrupted week, facilities are offered for reaching the open spaces of the outer fringe of London at a price within the reach of all but the destitute.'

The theme of using the Underground to escape from the smoke and grime of London is one that recurs in Edwardian Tube advertising in many forms. Posters depicted healthy-looking children walking down leafy country lanes or views of picture-postcard villages at the end of suburban lines. One version had a rabbit popping out of a rabbit-hole and saying to another 'Did you come by Underground?' Sometimes pictures of the gloomy city and contrasting bright countryside were juxtaposed (see the poster for Golders Green, plate 57) in an effective though some-what obvious way.

Travel through London by Underground for pleasure rather than just for getting to work was another theme much used in Tube advertising, sometimes with the addition of gentle humour. The quirky advertisement for the Central London Railway being as cool as a cucumber is a good example (plate 55), as is the magnet (plate 58) attracting hundreds of tiny figures into the underground system. With the advent of partial electrification, Tube travel was more pleasant and less dirty than before, though not without its problems. When the Inner Circle and Metropolitan and District Railway were first electrified in July 1905, electric and steam-hauled trains ran on the same lines at the same time and any electrical failure trapped steam trains between the electric ones.

By 1910 things had improved greatly and the *Railway Magazine* was able to comment 'electric haulage and automatic electric signalling have made it possible to run forty trains per hour at busy periods'. The Tube was promoted as the ideal means of clean and convenient transport for short pleasure trips to parks, museums, sporting facilities, exhibitions and so on. The Central London Railway, for example, produced several posters specially for the Franco-British Exhibition of 1908 (plate 52), which attracted hundreds of thousands of visitors, both British and foreign.

Edwardian transport posters were produced in response to the ever-growing market for holiday and leisure travel. The rail and shipping companies which commissioned them were making a deliberate appeal to the dreams of the travelling public, whether of a quick trip to the capital, a relaxing seaside or country holiday, or a long sea voyage to some exotic destination. The sometimes unsophisticated style of these posters is balanced by their clarity and directness. They became a picture gallery for everyone, a truly popular art form of the time.

A NOTE ON THE PLATES

The posters in this book form part of the archive held in the Public Record Office at Kew. They were folded up in boxes with their original copyright registration forms and hardly touched for the next eighty or ninety years. The folds are now so entrenched in the sometimes very fragile paper that it is difficult to smooth them out entirely to give a flat surface for photography. This explains the faintly three-dimensional effect visible in some of the plates. However, the silver lining of this cloud is that as the posters have been almost entirely protected from light, most of them are in excellent condition; their original colours have been extremely well preserved and they still appear as bright and glowing as the day they were printed.

INDEX TO ARTISTS

The Plates

View of Robin Hood's Bay from the Ravenscar Terraces.

PLATE 1

Ravenscar

North Eastern Railway

The windy North Yorkshire coast looks perfect here in this calm, sunny view across Robin Hood's Bay. Refreshing seaside air and healthy outdoor pursuits such as golf are the delights to tempt tourists to the tiny resort of Ravenscar, a station on the North Eastern Railway's coastal line. This style of poster is typical of the landscape-based designs so common in railway advertising of the period: upper and lower sections of densely packed headings and information, an almost photographically accurate view of the scenery, and the whole embellished with curlicues at top and bottom.

Artist: William Tomkin
Date: June 1909
Registered by: Waterlow & Sons Ltd
PRO reference: COPY 1/282 folio 118

PLATE 2

Great Western Railway

Weymouth

'Weymouth, the Naples of England' proudly proclaims this poster, with its wide sweep of pastel-hued bay aiming to conjure up a vision of the sunlit coast of southern Italy. Although the town used this slogan for years it is curiously inappropriate for anywhere marketed as a health resort as Naples was regarded as a picturesque but rather unhealthy spot by Edwardian society. Weymouth's heyday was at the end of the eighteenth century, when George III and his court developed a craze for sea-bathing and made a series of extended visits between 1789 and 1805, but after that the town faded into discreet gentility and had to rely on its beautiful bay and mild climate to attract visitors.

Artist: Alec Fraser
Date: July 1907
Registered by: Great Western Railway Co. Ltd
PRO reference: COPY 1/259i folio 261

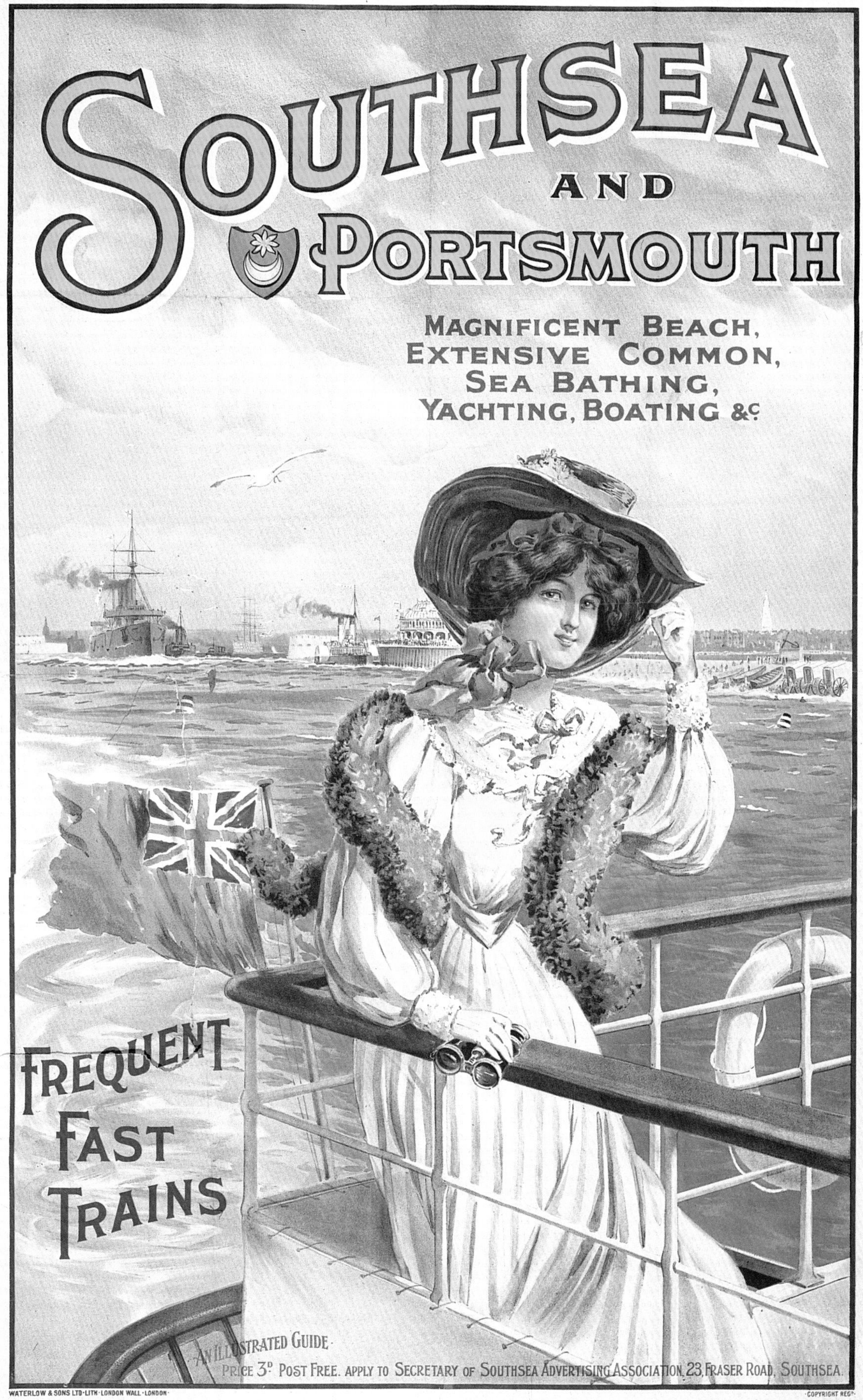

PLATE 3

Southsea and Portsmouth

This poster is slightly unusual in that it relies heavily on the image of an attractive woman for its impact, giving the design a faintly continental air: French travel posters of the period used the female form to a great extent but British ones relied far more on landscape than figures. The red ensign flying from the boat's rail and the Royal Navy warships in the background combine to give a hint of patriotism – who needs holidays abroad when you have good old British Southsea? The poster is also singular in that it was not published by one of the railway companies but for the Southsea Advertising Association.

Artist: John Hutton Walker
Date: July 1905
Registered by: Waterlow & Sons Ltd
PRO reference: COPY 1/231i folio 234

PLATE 4

Brighton and South Coast Railway

Summer Holidays

Who could resist the lure of a breezy holiday by the English Channel? The Brighton and South Coast Railway's promotional leaflet for 1905 says it all: 'With the delightful South Downs at the rear, the Sussex Seaside Towns are favourably situated. The rapid growth of these is sufficient testimony of the benefit and pleasure derived by past and present generations from a sojourn by the Silvery Sea, and the healthfulness of an admixture of sunshine and sea breezes.' Here they are adding proximity to France as a subliminal element too: we have the twin-screw turbine steamer *Brighton*, which regularly sailed on the Newhaven to Dieppe crossing from 1903 onwards, and a sailing boat registered in Dieppe, complete with Frenchmen in berets.

Artist: William Tomkin
Date: July 1905
Registered by: Waterlow & Sons Ltd
PRO reference: COPY 1/232 folio 522

**Great Yarmouth &
Gorleston-on-Sea**

A touch of holiday romance
is implied in this poster,
where a girl looks coyly away
from her admirer, twirling
her cherry-red parasol. Strict
Edwardian social rules were
relaxed a little away from
home and the consequent
slightly freer atmosphere was
an element of holiday travel
that advertisers felt they could
discreetly exploit.
Respectability is still
maintained, however – the
couple are in full public view
with several children nearby
on the sands. Great
Yarmouth, a long-established
and prosperous fishing port,
was fast becoming a very
popular resort, with a high
proportion of its visitors
drawn from the working
classes.

Artist: Frederick Hammersley
Ball
Date: May 1910
Registered by: Thomas
Forman & Sons, Nottingham
PRO reference: COPY 1/293i
folio 329

PLATE 6

Brighton Railway

For Isle of Wight

Much of the advertising for the Isle of Wight concentrated on yachting, but this one does so only obliquely in the form of the naval officer. This poster, like plate 5, offers a subtle hint of the greater social licence associated with travel and holidays; the young man uses his telescope to eye the woman and girl promenading on the shore. The colours are soft and attractive, and with the large areas of even tint, free of fussy detail, the artist has produced a clear, vivid design.

Artist: Helen Legard
Date: June 1903
Registered by: Waterlow & Sons Ltd
PRO reference: COPY 1/204 folio 135

PLATE 7

London & South Western Railway

Weymouth

It is interesting to compare this poster with plate 2, also an advertisement for Weymouth. Here we have two railway companies in direct competition with each other for the lucrative holiday traffic, approaching the problem of how to attract passengers by means of two entirely different styles of poster art. One might guess that this poster is dated much later than the Great Western Railway one, but in fact it predates it by three years. We can only conclude that the Great Western Railway were innately resistant to change as their favoured style of advertising remained very much the same from the late Victorian period right up to the First World War. The London & South Western Railway had a far more innovative advertising department, exemplified by this memorable picture of the girl pensively musing as she feeds the swans at her feet.

Artist: Adrianne Loder (trading as 'Adrian')
Date: February 1904
Registered by: Waterlow & Sons Ltd
PRO reference: COPY 1/213 folio 272

PLATE 8

Great Northern Railway

John Hassall's posters for the Great Northern Railway show a real sense of humour and lightness of touch. The original copyright registration form for this delightful advertisement describes it as 'a drawing of a gouty invalid with one foot bandaged, laughing and jumping with joy, pulling a bath chair attendant over the sands at Sea Side in his own chair'. It is an amusing image, guaranteed to make the traveller feel well disposed towards the Great Northern Railway and its east coast destinations. The large areas of flat colour – bright blue sky and yellow sand – and contrasting small touches of red, orange, black and white give it a similar character to Hassall's more famous poster 'Skegness is so bracing'. It was later overprinted with information about the three-shilling cheap day returns to Skegness.

Artist: John Hassall
Date: June 1911
Registered by: Johnson, Riddle & Co. Ltd and the Great Northern Railway Co. Ltd
PRO reference: COPY 1/310 folio 414

PLATE 9

Great Northern Railway

Here we have a poster for the Great Northern Railway dating from 1904, seven years before Hassall's gentleman with the bath chair. The theme this time is the family holiday with the children happily paddling at the water's edge. The wide sands of the east coast resorts were frequently promoted as a paradise for children and posters for Scarborough, Great Yarmouth, Mablethorpe in Lincolnshire and the north Kent towns such as Margate and Broadstairs all feature boys and girls playing on the beach with buckets and spades.

Artist: John Hayes
Date: June 1904
Registered by: Great Northern Railway Co. Ltd
PRO reference: COPY 1/217i folio 218

GREAT NORTHERN RAILWAY

FOR PARTICULARS OF TOURIST, WEEK-END AND OTHER CHEAP TICKETS, APPLY AT ANY GREAT NORTHERN STATION OR TOWN OFFICE.

DESIGNED & PRINTED BY A.VIVIAN MANSELL & Co LONDON & MANCHESTER

OLIVER BURY, General Manager.

PLATE 10

London & South Western Railway

Swanage

Perceptions of what constitutes an attractive child have obviously changed over the years. This Little Lord Fauntleroy of the sands was an image of the ideal child to Edwardian parents – clean, tidy, not a speck of sand or water on him right down to the fluffy bobbles on his shoes. The glorious sweep of beach with families dotted here and there on it is clearly intended to appeal to parents looking for a suitable spot for a family holiday. An interesting sideline is that this is one of the very few Edwardian posters still to show bathing machines. In many resorts they had already disappeared by the turn of the century, but Swanage was always regarded as a rather staid and old-fashioned place – no casinos or bright lights – so they may well have lingered on for years.

Artist: William Tomkin
Date: October 1908
Registered by: Waterlow & Sons Ltd
PRO reference: COPY 1/275 folio 371

Midland Railway

The New Route to the Isle of Man

The Isle of Man had been popular for seaside holidays since the middle of the nineteenth century, especially for citizens of the north-west and the Potteries. In Arnold Bennett's *Anna of the Five Towns* (1902), Anna, like all travellers to the island, sees it for the first time from the ferry: 'There, a morsel in the waste of the deep, a speck under the infinite sunlight, lay the island, mysterious, enticing, enchanted, a glinting jewel on the sea's bosom, a remote entity fraught with strange secrets.' By the Edwardian era the island was linked to the mainland by several steamer services and in 1905 the Midland Railway opened a new one from Heysham, advertised here in a bright, cheerful poster showing the *Manxman* steaming out of its own lifebelt surrounded by bright blue sea and sky.

Artist: Herbert Steventon
Date: May 1905
Registered by: David Browne & Co., Nottingham
PRO reference: COPY 1/229ii folio 131

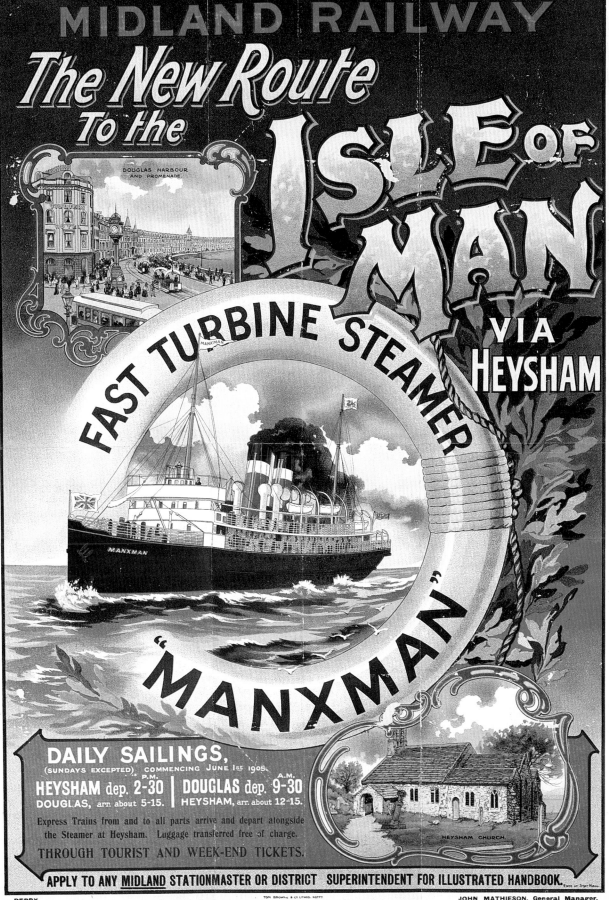

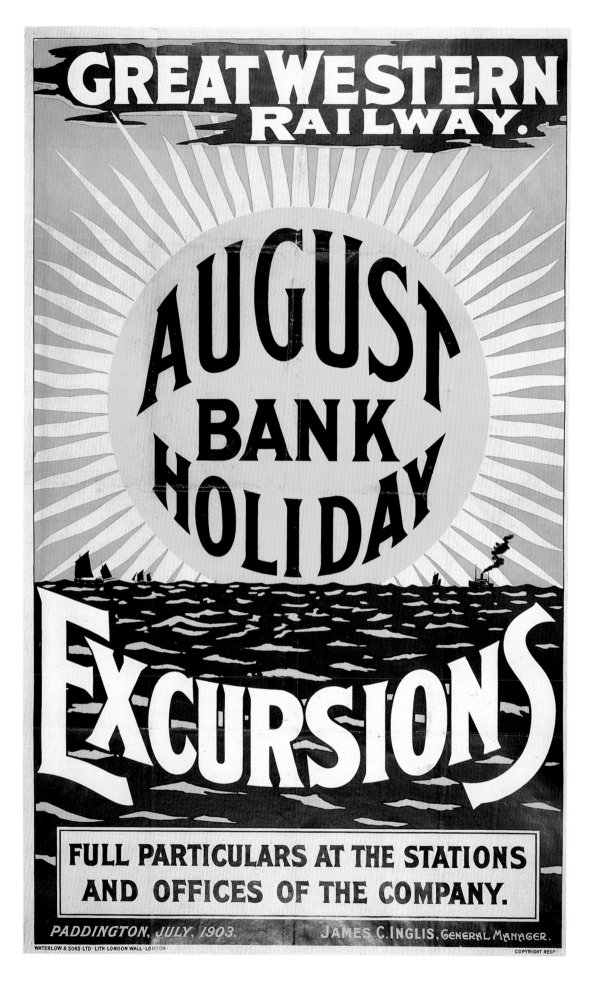

PLATE 12

Great Western Railway

August Bank Holiday
Excursions

This is the ultimate in bold, conspicuous images where the idea behind the poster is simply to force the observer to see and remember it, rather than to convey specific information. Wouldn't we all like a vast hot sun to shine out of a bright blue sky on August Bank Holiday? And of course a Great Western Railway excursion would be exactly the sort of trip to fulfil the desire for a day out by the sea.

Artist: George Conning
Date: July 1903
Registered by: Waterlow & Sons Ltd
PRO reference: COPY 1/205 folio 199

PLATE 13

Great Northern Railway

Whitsuntide Excursions

Another enormous sun, this time setting in a warm golden glow over the waves and illuminating the family on the cliff top, enjoying the last of their day at the seaside. This poster and the next (plate 14) are among several designed at much the same time for the Great Northern Railway by Edward Sharland. A minor curiosity in these is that there appears to be no distinctive house style of lettering for the company – on each of these examples he has used a different typeface, and it is different again on Great Northern Railway posters by other artists (see plates 8 and 9). Some companies were far more consistent (see, for instance, the Midland Railway posters, plates 32, 36, 50 and 51).

Artist: Edward Sharland
Date: May 1904
Registered by: Waterlow & Sons Ltd
PRO reference: COPY 1/216 folio 406

GREAT NORTHERN RAILWAY.

WHITSUNTIDE EXCURSIONS

FOR PARTICULARS OF EXCURSION ARRANGEMENTS SEE SMALL BILLS

Obtainable at the Company's Stations & Offices.

LONDON · KING'S CROSS · APRIL · 1904 ·   OLIVER BURY, GENERAL MANAGER.

WATERLOW & SONS LTD · DUNSTABLE · & LONDON ·   COPYRIGHT · REGD

PLATE 14

Great Northern Railway

Christmas and New Year Holidays

This delightful winter scene of boys sliding on a snowy slope has a wonderful Christmassy air. The main picture is very simply designed in black and white but the touches of red in the scarf, hat and holly berries make all the difference, picking up the bright scarlet lettering of the company's name and Father Christmas's hooded coat. The Great Northern Railway was pre-eminent in the number of excursions it ran in the summer months and attempted to retain passenger loyalty with reduced fares and special trips over Christmas.

Artist: Edward Sharland
Date: November 1903
Registered by: Waterlow & Sons Ltd
PRO reference: COPY 1/209 folio 264

PLATE 15

Great Western Railway

Xmas Excursions

The Great Western Railway was as keen as the Great Northern to encourage train excursions over the Christmas period. All the railway companies put much emphasis on the joys of being back in the bosom of the family at Christmas-time and many of their advertisements showed people round a heavily laden table, with food and drink figuring strongly. The footman carrying in an enormous pudding is a neat variation on this theme. The red, black and dark brown against yellow, the brightest possible background, make a very noticeable combination of colours and would stand out well in any collection of advertising material.

Artist: George Conning
Date: November 1903
Registered by: Waterlow & Sons Ltd
PRO reference: COPY 1/209 folio 47

GREAT WESTERN RAILWAY.

XMAS

EXCURSIONS

TO CORNWALL THE RIVIERA OF ENGLAND

TO NORTH & SOUTH WALES

TO THE DORSET COAST

AND OTHER PARTS OF THE LINE

FULL PARTICULARS AT THE STATIONS AND OFFICES OF THE COMPANY.

PADDINGTON STATION. DECEMBER

JAMES C. INGLIS General Manager.

WATERLOW & SONS LTD·LITH·

COPYRIGHT REGD

PLATE 16

New Pullman Express
The Southern Belle

This magnificent drawing-room carriage is the epitome of true first-class travel, with its thick carpet, lavish decoration, proper movable armchairs and refreshments always to hand. First-class travel today is a poor substitute for Edwardian luxury! From 2 November 1908 the Brighton Railway ran a daily service of all-Pullman cars in addition to their usual trains, aiming firmly at the top of the market as we can see from the elegantly clad women depicted here in their vast hats and fur stoles. The service quickly became so popular that from 1 June 1909 two trips were made in each direction every day.

Artist: Edward Sharland
Date: February 1909
Registered by: Waterlow & Sons Ltd
PRO reference: COPY 1/278 folio 101

PLATE 17

London Brighton & South Coast Railway

Coast Line Rail Motor Services

This single-carriage train with its steam boiler at the front looks almost too good to be true – it could be an illustration lifted straight out of a children's story. In fact it really did exist – it is another element of the services provided by the London, Brighton and South Coast Railway, very different from their first-class Pullman travel to Brighton. Here we see the train trundling past a golf course and the ruins of Pevensey Castle on the Sussex coast.

Artist: William Tomkin
Date: April 1906
Registered by: Waterlow & Sons Ltd
PRO reference: COPY 1/243ii folio 151

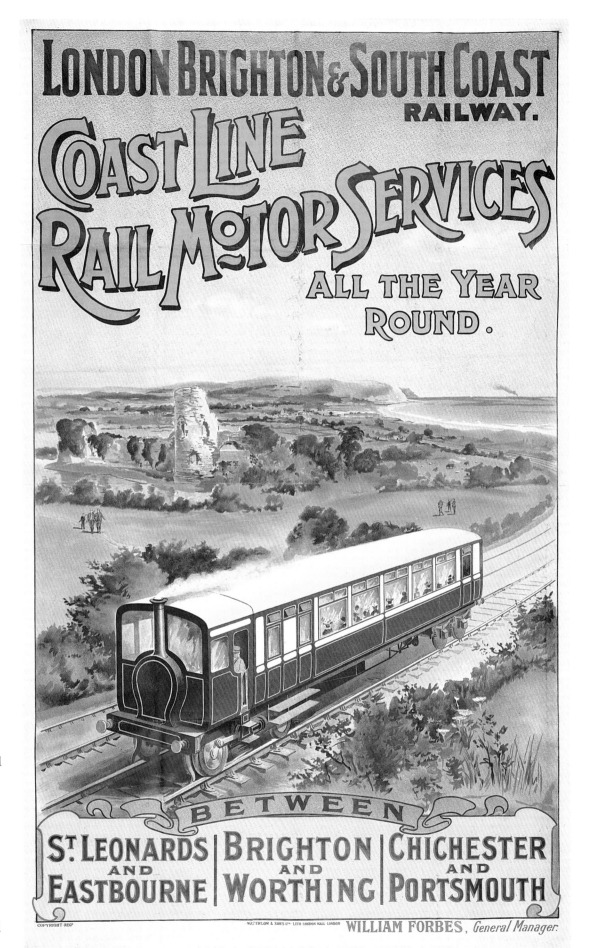

PLATE 18

Brighton Railway

Sussex Downs

Just occasionally the cool, clean, family-orientated image of railway travel slips a little: the girl holding her milking stool throws a wistful glance towards the lad further down the hill and we begin to wonder what romantic possibilities the Sussex Downs might hold in a day or weekend trip. The appeal here is a good deal more subtle in both content and style than in many railway posters – in particular the colours are much softer and more harmonious than the usual bright tones and high contrasts. Perhaps it is significant that the graphic artist in this case was one of the few women in the field.

Artist: Agnes Joseph
Date: July 1903
Registered by: Waterlow & Sons Ltd
PRO reference: COPY 1/205 folio 289

PLATE 19

Furness Railway

New Steam Yacht 'Lady of the Lake'

'Travellers by the Furness Railway will not fail to notice the very artistic posters with which the stations are decorated,' commented the *Railway and Travel Monthly* in August 1910. This is a particularly pretty one, showing Coniston Lake with a rather voluptuous young woman on the hillside waving her handkerchief towards the pleasure steamer *Lady of the Lake* moored at the jetty below. The steamer was newly built for the Furness Railway in 1908, when this poster was commissioned, as part of their extensive programme of combined rail and boat excursions in the spring and summer.

Artist: William Tomkin
Date: April 1908
Registered by: Waterlow & Sons Ltd
PRO reference: COPY 1/268 folio 30

PLATE 20

Great Western Railway

Motor Service between Marlborough and Calne

The Great Western Railway operated a number of motor bus services to link up with the railway (see also the New Quay poster, plate 30). The Marlborough to Calne bus through the depths of Wiltshire was one of these, winding through the country lanes loaded with the usual vast Edwardian quantity of trunks and boxes. The heavy emphasis on text in this poster recalls the old railway handbills of the nineteenth century, but the addition of colour, though limited in this example, gives much greater impact.

Artist: George Conning
Date: October 1904
Registered by: Waterlow & Sons Ltd
PRO reference: COPY 1/222 folio 1

PLATE 21

Great Western Railway

Hunting Season

The Great Western Railway's publicity department may not have been in the forefront of new trends in graphic design but it was certainly not slow to make use of any possibilities in the calendar for special trips, lower fares for limited periods, or other promotional ideas. Bank Holidays, Christmas, Easter, the polo season and river regattas were all good reasons for arranging excursions – as was the hunting season, promoted here. The decorative details are very apt – stirrups and riding crops are incorporated into the information labels. A nice touch is that horses as well as grooms were eligible for reduced fares!

Artist: William Tomkin
Date: September 1903
Registered by: Waterlow & Sons Ltd
PRO reference: COPY 1/207 folio 277

GREAT WESTERN RAILWAY.

HUNTING SEASON·

HUNTING SEASON TICKETS.

GROOMS. REDUCED FARES

HORSES. REDUCED RATES.

FULL PARTICULARS AT THE STATIONS AND OFFICES OF THE COMPANY.

PADDINGTON STATION.

JAMES C. INGLIS, General Manager.

WATERLOW & SONS, LTD LITH. LONDON WALL, LONDON.

COPYRIGHT REGᴰ

PLATE 22

South Eastern & Chatham Railway

Sunny Broadstairs

'Hurrah! at Broadstairs,' in the words of Mr Pooter in *Diary of a Nobody* (1892). He and his family had an unfortunately cool and overcast trip there a week after the August Bank Holiday – quite the opposite of the ideal picture of warmth and sunshine in this advertisement commissioned by the Broadstairs Advancement and Protection Association. Broadstairs and the other north Kent resorts served by the South Eastern and Chatham Railway were popular for day and weekend excursions because of their nearness to London and their advertising was aimed squarely at the family market. Second-class carriages were still retained by the railway company at this period. This is an effective design except that the clouds appear to be hewn out of the same solid chalk as the cliffs.

Artist: William Lasham
Date: April 1909
Registered by: Broadstairs Advancement and Protection Association
PRO reference: COPY 1/280 folio 142

PLATE 23

London Tilbury & Southend Railway

Southend & Westcliff-on-Sea

Southend-sur-Mer? The strong blue sky, truly sea-green sea and touches of brilliant white, red and yellow glow with heat and light, producing an almost Mediterranean atmosphere. In 1862 the author of *The Railway Traveller's Handbook* regarded the place as 'calm and quiet, especially suitable for the debilitated frame and the harassed mind'! A few years later he would hardly have recognised it. The census of 1871 recorded a population of less than 3000, but by 1911 it had ballooned to nearly 63,000 and the town had become an enormously popular resort, especially for day-trippers from London. The railway company's advertising manager was even then dealing in fantasy to attract the holidaymaker: this smooth sweep of shoreline, almost empty of figures, was just as much an unattainable ideal in 1909 as it would be on a busy Bank Holiday today.

Artist: Edward Sharland
Date: June 1909
Registered by: Waterlow & Sons Ltd
PRO reference: COPY 1/282 folio 123

PLATE 24

Underground

Too Much of a Good Thing

This illustrates well the plethora of possibilities offered to the family looking for a day out. It can also be seen as a wry comment on the vast rise in the number of advertisements on public view everywhere by the end of the Edwardian period. The posters on the wall are not merely figments of the artist's imagination but real contemporary ones, used as part of the unified Underground advertising campaign begun in 1911. Curiously the one at the far right is not an Underground poster like the rest but one for the London, Tilbury and Southend Railway (see plate 23).

Artist: John Henry Lloyd
Date: March 1911
Registered by: Johnson, Riddle & Co. Ltd
PRO reference: COPY 1/305 folio 84

PLATE 25

Great Western Railway

See Your Own Country First

The Great Western Railway have here departed from their usual style and produced something a little different. This clever visual joke makes an attractive and humorous design: the maps, young women and fruit are neatly paired and the comparison even extends to the copy-lines about the Greeks and Romans. It was a particularly successful poster and in addition to the versions such as this, printed on paper for railway hoardings, it was also reproduced on enamel sheet, a technique usually employed for advertising consumer products with enduring appeal (beer or Marmite, for example).

Artist: Arthur Gunn
Date: April 1907
Registered by: Johnson, Riddle & Co. Ltd
PRO reference: COPY 1/256 folio 141

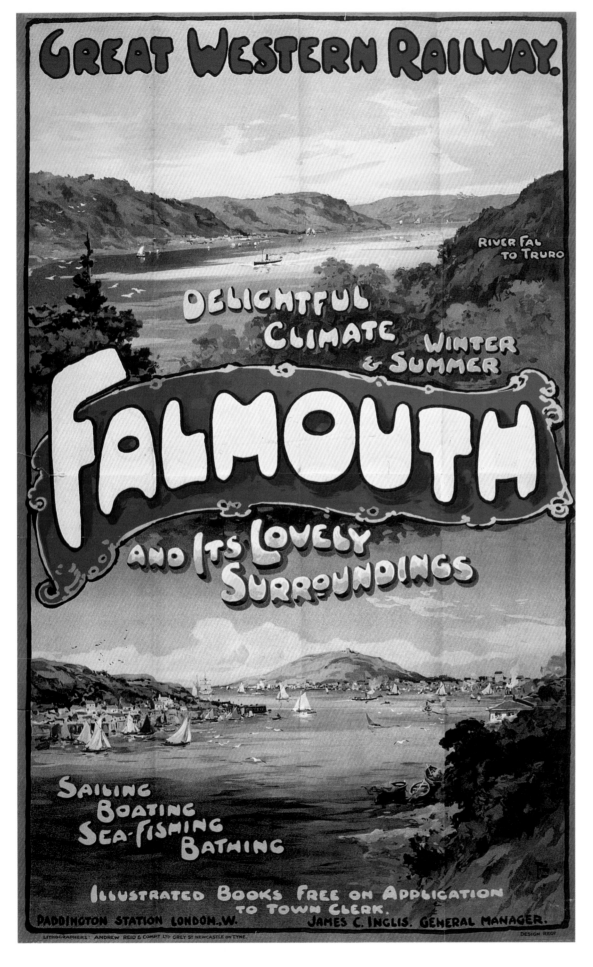

PLATE 26

Great Western Railway

Falmouth

This is a fine example of the traditional picture-postcard type of poster favoured for years by the rather conservative advertising department of the Great Western Railway: two bright and attractive scenes, separated by a curved banner proclaiming the town's name in large, solid, rounded lettering. It was designed by Frederick Simpson, who produced a large number of posters at this time for the Great Western Railway and other companies (see also plates 34 and 40). Being a long distance from almost anywhere, Falmouth was always regarded as a relatively exclusive resort and the emphasis here is firmly on scenery and climate rather than on artificial attractions of mass appeal.

Artist: Frederick Simpson
Date: June 1907
Registered by: Andrew Reid & Co.
PRO reference: COPY 1/258 folio 322

PLATE 27

Great Western Railway

Trips on the Dart and Fal Rivers

A delightful view of the River Fal in Cornwall is depicted on this poster, with a pleasure steamer cruising gently past a landing stage and houses nestling against the steeply sloping bank. The Great Western Railway promoted their south-western holiday destinations primarily in terms of landscape and natural beauty and arranged a programme of river excursions to complement their train trips, doing their utmost to prevent passengers deserting them for rival attractions.

Artist: William Tomkin
Date: July 1903
Registered by: Waterlow & Sons Ltd
PRO reference: COPY 1/205 folio 237

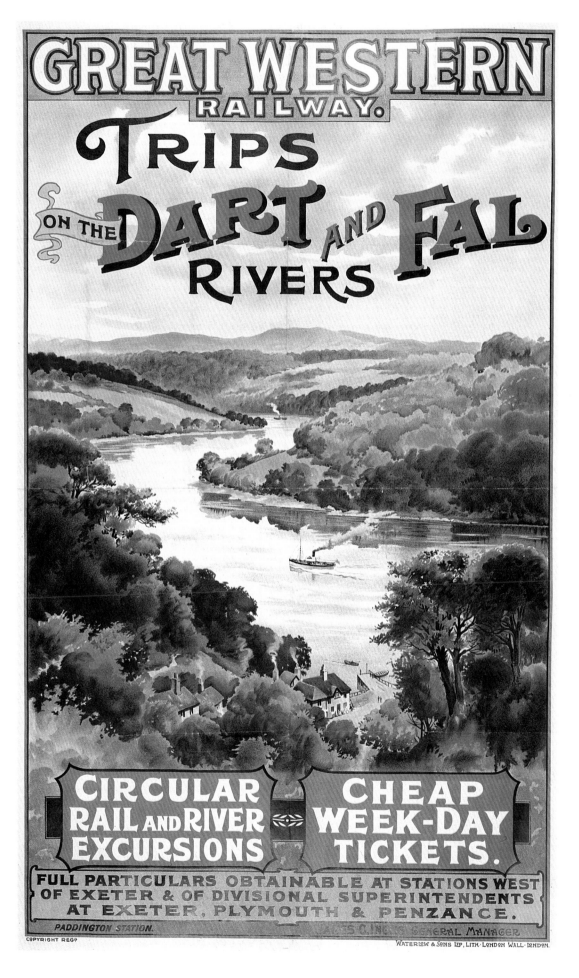

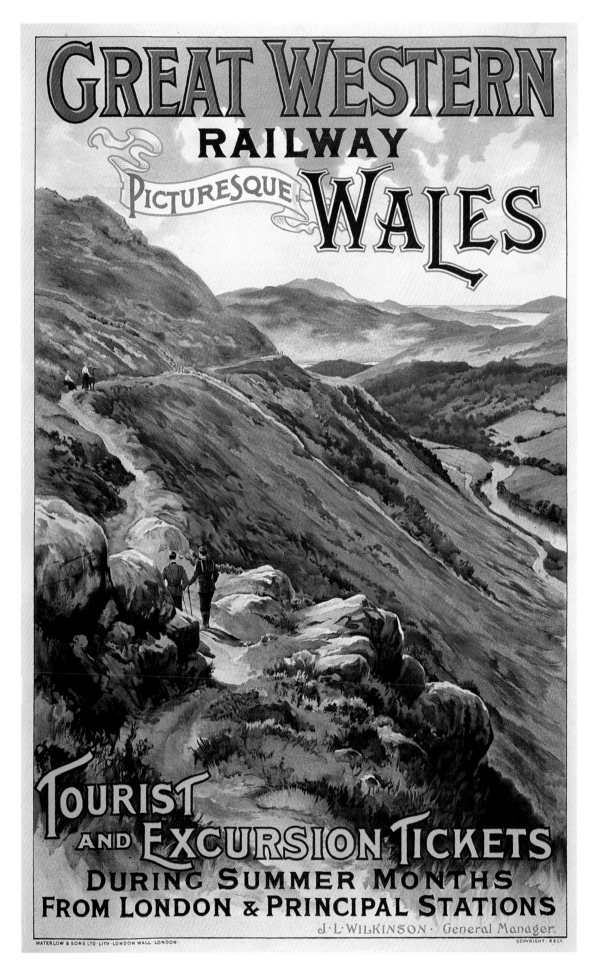

PLATE 28

Great Western Railway

Picturesque Wales

This attractive view of the
precipice walk near Dolgellau
is another painting by
William Tomkin very similar
in atmosphere to his
advertisement for the Dart
and Fal trips (plate 27). Both
are absolutely standard
posters of the traditional
landscape type, relying heavily
on the beauty of the scenery
rather than on any innovation
in design. Here the walkers in
their sturdy Norfolk jackets,
plus fours and caps exemplify
the sort of holidaymakers at
whom the poster is aimed:
admirers of the countryside,
free to wander at will, rather
than families bound for the
seaside.

Artist: William Tomkin
Date: June 1902
Registered by: Waterlow
& Sons Ltd
PRO reference: COPY 1/191
folio 45

PLATE 29

Great Western Railway

Tenby

The clashing hints of yellow, orange and red and the thick, 'bubble' style of lettering frequently employed by Alec Fraser for extra emphasis make this poster look surprisingly modern. The name 'Tenby' itself stands out especially well even though surrounded by a mass of lettering which obscures the greater part of the picture. Tenby was promoted by the Great Western Railway as a health resort offering relaxed outdoor pursuits such as golfing and fishing. Originally a prosperous fishing port, by 1900 it increasingly depended on its new-found popularity for seaside holidays.

Artist: Alec Fraser
Date: June 1905
Registered by: Great Western Railway Co. Ltd
PRO reference: COPY 1/230 folio 202

PLATE 30

Great Western Railway
New Quay, Cardiganshire

The Great Western Railway management realised the value of providing their own motor-bus services as feeders to the railway, particularly from small seaside towns without stations of their own. Here is the New Quay bus service from Llandyssil, crammed with holidaymakers and an excess of luggage, like the Wiltshire bus in plate 20. This is another design by Alec Fraser, rather more conventional than plate 29, but still with his favourite solid lettering, especially effective here as the GWR initials.

Artist: Alec Fraser
Date: January 1908
Registered by: Great Western Railway Co. Ltd
PRO reference: COPY 1/265 folio 368

PLATE 31

Midland Railway

The Most Interesting Route to Scotland

An enormous bird, probably a black cock which was a popular game bird in the Highlands, dominates this rather strange poster for travel by the Midland Railway to Scotland. The various companies were in hot competition to gain a good slice of the market and it was possible to travel north by several different routes either via the east coast, the west coast or inland up the backbone of England as this route map advertises.

Artist: Alfred Nicholls
Date: July 1907
Registered by: Nathaniel Lloyd & Co.
PRO reference: COPY 1/259ii folio 18

PLATE 32

Midland Railway

Scotland and the North of England

Hoots mon! This caricature of a Scotsman, complete with sporran, red beard and matching nose, was designed to appeal to the prejudices of English people at the time, whose view of Scotland as nothing but kilts and whisky this poster appears to reinforce. It would be interesting to discover whether this was regarded as an effective advertisement or not: presumably the Midland Railway (in conjunction with Thomas Cook) thought that such an image would encourage people to visit Scotland to view the 'natives' for themselves. By contrast, most of the other posters promoting Scotland relied on well-known Scottish landmarks for their appeal.

Artist: Andrew Murray
Date: October 1904
Registered by: David Allen & Sons
PRO reference: COPY 1/221 folio 245

PLATE 33

David MacBrayne Ltd

Summer Tours in the Western Highlands and Islands

Royal route, Royal Mail steamers, even a large crown which appears to be hovering over the waves: the MacBrayne Steamship Company are exploiting royal associations here to the limit. The *Columba* and her sister ship the *Iona* both carried the mail as well as vast numbers of holidaymakers: they sailed from Glasgow every day to Rothesay and through the Kyles of Bute to Tarbert and Ardrishaig. The *Railway and Travel Monthly* of June 1911 was surprised to find the *Columba* used in advertising material because she was built in 1878 and 'though she was undoubtedly a fine vessel in her day, she must now be called rather out of date.' The writer also noted that over 200,000 items of Royal Mail per month passed through the post office on board the *Columba*.

Artist: Joseph Carey
Date: September 1907
Registered by: David MacBrayne Ltd
PRO reference: COPY 1/261 folio 319

PLATE 34

Great Western Railway

The Direct Route to Ireland

There was a good deal of competition for Irish ferry traffic between the railway companies. In the summer of 1906 the Great Western Railway opened a new ferry port at Fishguard in South Wales from which a steamer service sailed regularly to Rosslare in County Wexford, formerly just a small fishing village. The harbour at Rosslare was also reconstructed and enlarged to accommodate the ferries. This dramatic painting of the *St Patrick*, bows-on with the sun setting low behind her, is a strong, simple image which puts across the idea of the ferry service very effectively. It would stand out well among the mass of posters usually on display at railway stations.

Artist: Frederick Simpson
Date: March 1906
Registered by: Great Western Railway Co. Ltd
PRO reference: COPY 1/242i folio 330

PLATE 35

Great Western Railway

Cheap Fares, Fast Trains and Steamers to Southern Ireland

The intrepid traveller has boarded the steamer, crossed the Irish Sea, and is now confronted by the impressive fifteenth-century keep of Blarney Castle near Cork. The Great Western Railway put a good deal of effort into promoting southern Ireland, particularly the Cork and Wexford areas, as a holiday destination for lovers of quiet walks and fine scenery. This poster by Alec Fraser, full of his trademark greens and browns with a glowing sunset to lighten it, is one of their most notable.

Artist: Alec Fraser
Date: August 1904
Registered by: Great Western Railway Co. Ltd
PRO reference: COPY 1/219i folio 102

PLATE 36

Midland Railway

Cook's Excursions to Ireland

This dramatic design in two colours only is one of a series of magnificent posters produced for the Midland Railway by the printers and advertising agents David Allen and Sons in 1904 (see also the London posters, plates 50 and 51). It demonstrates well the 'less is more' theory of poster design. How much clearer and more memorable is this uncluttered image than one of the busy advertisements crammed with superfluous detail such as the one shown in plate 37. It represents Carrick-a-Rede on the coast of County Antrim, where a hazardous rope bridge eighty feet above the waves spanned the chasm between the rocky islet and the mainland. The blank space at the bottom was left for later overprinting of excursion details or whatever announcement was deemed necessary, a frequent practice that ensured the speedy dissemination of publicity.

Artist: Dennis Fitzsimmons
Date: October 1904
Registered by: David Allen & Sons
PRO reference: COPY 1/221 folio 269

PLATE 37

H. McNeill Ltd

How to Spend a Cheap Holiday in the North of Ireland

The northern counties of Ireland were promoted as a holiday area primarily in terms of their splendid coastal landscape. This is another poster produced by the advertising firm of David Allen and Sons, like plate 36, but this time by their Belfast branch rather than the London head office. They were clearly light-years behind in the provinces in terms of striking design but this is nevertheless attractive. The artist has made good use of the Irish shamrock symbol, with the large central outline neatly gathering the four County Antrim scenes together and the motif repeated in miniature all round the edge.

Artist: Fred Williams
Date: June 1909
Registered by: David Allen & Sons Ltd, Belfast
PRO reference: COPY 1/282 folio 315

PLATE 38

South Eastern & Chatham Railway

Cook's Conducted Tours

This smart lady and her two gentlemen companions epitomise the comfortably-off upper classes and bourgeoisie at whom this advertisement is aimed. But the genuine aristocracy would not have considered going on a package tour: 'Switzerland and the Tyrol, and even Italy, are all redolent of Mr. Cook', according to Anthony Trollope. By 1900 Thomas Cook and Son were making arrangements for travellers all round the world but the greater part of their business was still in Europe, with passengers usually setting off from Victoria station via the South Eastern and Chatham Railway's boat-train service to the Channel ports.

Artist: Dennis Fitzsimmons
Date: October 1904
Registered by: David Allen & Sons
PRO reference: COPY 1/221 folio 247

Great Western Railway

Brest à Londres

The Great Western Railway wasted no opportunities for advertising – here it is promoting its cross-Channel ferry services on the French side of the water. This rather curious image of a Breton fisherman and Scottish highlander dancing hand-in-hand on the quayside uses a contemporary political slogan, in use in both France and Britain at the time, to reinforce the company's message. The *entente cordiale* signified the newly friendly relationship between the two countries which arose soon after the end of the Boer War in 1902. It was strongly fostered by Edward VII, always a francophile, and was to culminate in the alliance of 1914.

Artist: Alec Fraser
Date: August 1908
Registered by: Great Western Railway Co. Ltd
PRO reference: COPY 1/272 folio 61

PLATE 40

P&O

Round-the-World Tours

The dazzling glare and stupefying heat of the Orient are well evoked in the light, bright colours and sharply defined details of this attractive poster. The 'Moorish scene, native boat and palms in foreground', as the original registration document describes it, give a taste of the exotic destinations served by P&O's steamships. In 1905, when this poster was published, P&O maintained sixty-three vessels in its fleet and operated services to the Mediterranean, Middle East, India, Far East, Australia and New Zealand. From early 1910 they took over the Blue Anchor Line and so ran a service to South Africa as well.

Artist: Frederick Simpson
Date: June 1905
Registered by: Andrew Reid & Co. Ltd, Newcastle-on-Tyne
PRO reference: COPY 1/230 folio 184

PLATE 41

Great Indian Peninsula Railway

Poona Races

This poster is one of the very few to use the image of the train itself. The comfort of passengers was clearly the best selling point of the service and there is a mass of information describing the features of the train. The poster is reminiscent (at least in the lower half) of the old handbills that were the original type of railway advertising, with details of departure and arrival times, fares, arrangements for dining and so on. The passengers were obviously seen as belonging to the upper classes – the lower orders were kept firmly at a distance in a separate train service half an hour earlier, no doubt partly so that the servants (third class) were there ready to see to the needs of their masters at the other end, once they had arrived at the race-course.

Artist: Edward Sharland
Date: November 1905
Registered by: Waterlow & Sons Ltd
PRO reference: COPY 1/235ii folio 29

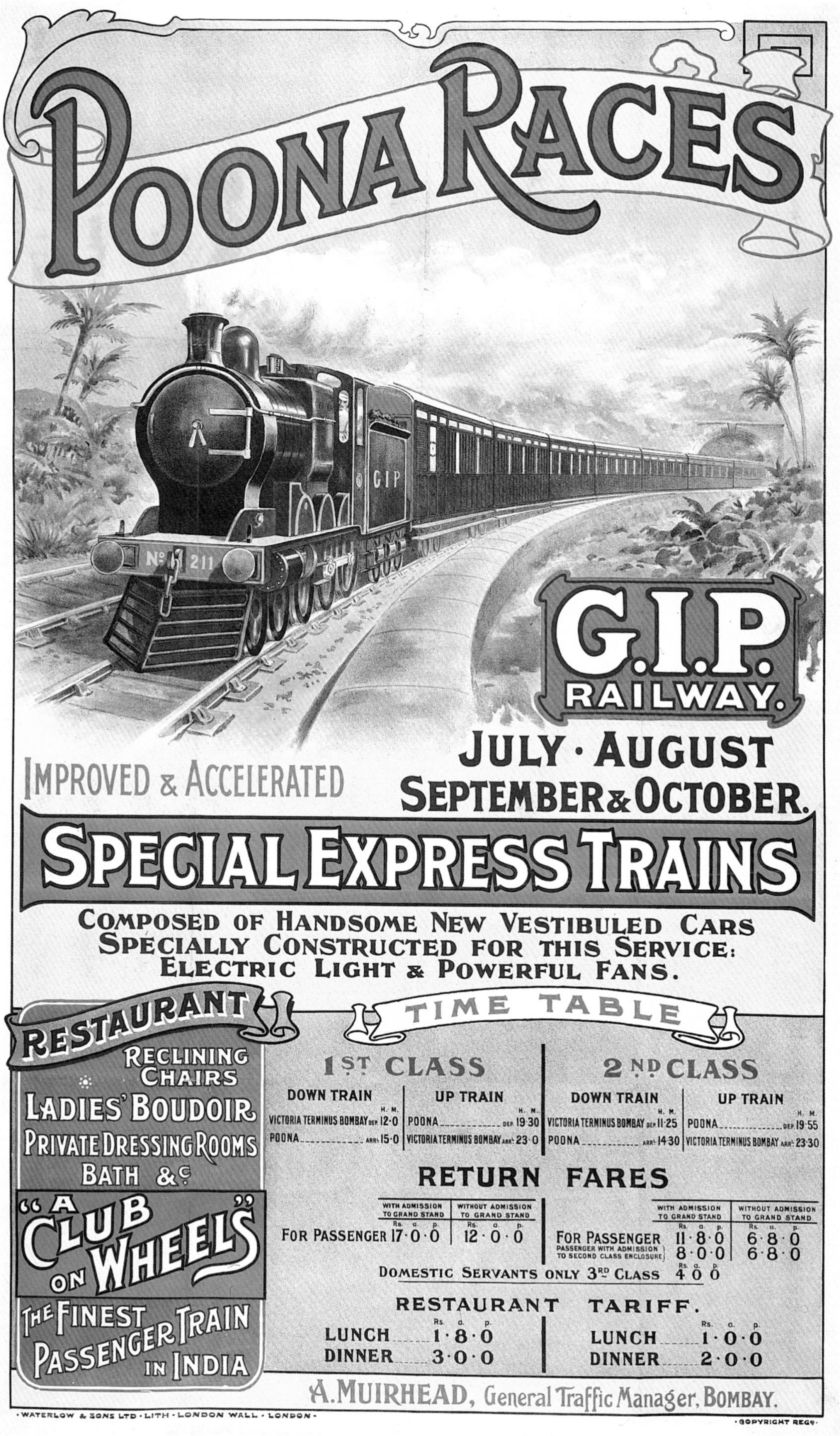

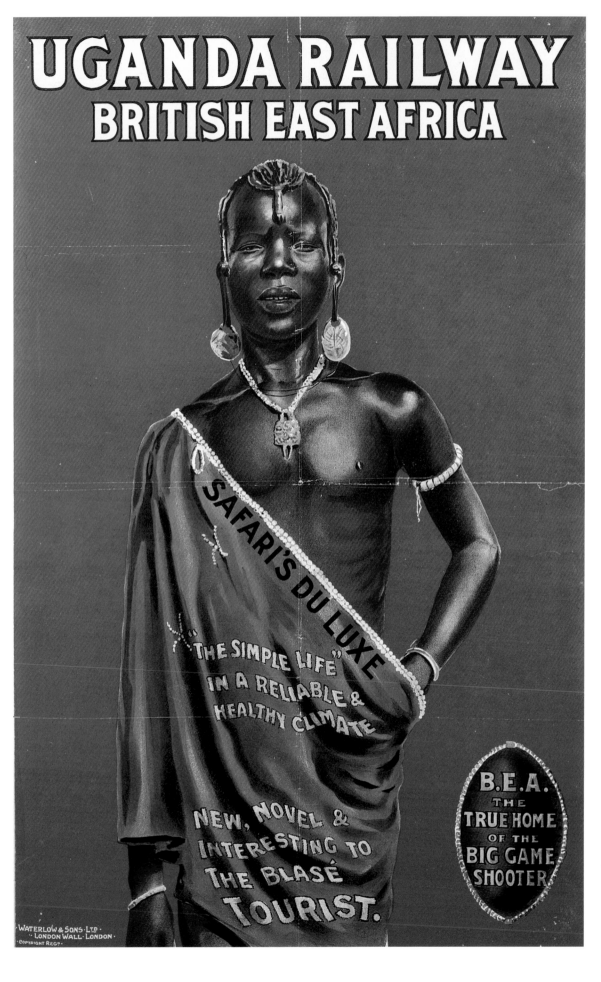

UGANDA RAILWAY
BRITISH EAST AFRICA

SAFARI'S DU LUXE

"THE SIMPLE LIFE" IN A RELIABLE & HEALTHY CLIMATE

NEW, NOVEL & INTERESTING TO THE BLASÉ TOURIST.

B.E.A. THE TRUE HOME OF THE BIG GAME SHOOTER

WATERLOW & SONS LTD · LONDON WALL · LONDON · COPYRIGHT REGD

PLATE 42

Uganda Railway

British East Africa

This exotic African figure with his green robe and gold jewellery is clearly designed to appeal as something 'new, novel and interesting to the blasé tourist' who has seen the rest of what the world has to offer. More and more travellers were beginning to look further afield and Africa was opening up as a place for holidays as well as for subduing the natives. Colonial railways, built originally as a means of communication in military, administrative and business matters, were now used for leisure and pleasure as well. Big game shooting was the biggest attraction.

Artist: Edward Sharland
Date: August 1908
Registered by: Waterlow & Sons Ltd
PRO reference: COPY 1/272 folio 217

PLATE 43

Uganda Railway

Step by Step Through Nature's "Zoo"

The Uganda Railway actually ran through British East Africa (now Kenya), not Uganda. Here we have a bird's-eye view of the railway as a series of steps (flanked by the usual telegraph poles) leading up to the central African plateau and Lake Victoria. The lion baring its teeth on a rock in the foreground is the pivot of the advertisement: interest in wildlife was certainly an element of tourism at the time, even though it may most often have been a case of 'If it moves, shoot it' – with a gun rather than camera.

Artist: Edward Sharland, according to the original registration form, but the poster is signed Bert Longworth.
Date: October 1908
Registered by: Waterlow & Sons Ltd
PRO reference: COPY 1/275 folio 370

THE IMPERIAL DIRECT
WEST INDIA MAIL SERVICE Co Ltd

"ARRIVAL OF AN IMPERIAL DIRECT WEST INDIA
MAIL STEAMER AT THE WEST INDIES."

REGULAR FORTNIGHTLY SAILINGS
TO AND FROM **JAMAICA** AND AVONMOUTH (BRISTOL)
ALSO TO BERMUDA EVERY SIX WEEKS

ELDER, DEMPSTER & Co. COLONIAL HOUSE. LIVERPOOL.
& AT CANADA HOUSE. BRISTOL. 4. St MARY AXE. LONDON. E.C.
30. MOSLEY St. MANCHESTER. CARDIFF. HAMBURG. Etc.

PLATE 44

**The Imperial Direct West
India Mail Service Co. Ltd**

The pink sunset reflected in
the ripples of water gives a
warm and welcoming
atmosphere to this poster for
one of the smaller shipping
lines of the period, whose
main trade was in freight and
mail but carried passengers
too. The small boat in the
foreground with the local
inhabitants and their bananas,
contrasting with the bulk of
the steamer behind, is clearly
meant to reinforce the
impression of a friendly
foreign shore. Jamaica was
beginning to open up to
tourist travel at this time, as
were several of the larger
islands of the Caribbean.

Artist: Ernest North
Date: September 1907
Registered by: Elder,
Dempster & Co., Liverpool
PRO reference: COPY 1/261
folio 159

PLATE 45

Dominion Line

Liverpool to Canada

This delightful scene of the
main deck of a steamer
looking aft gives us a rosy
picture of the North Atlantic
crossing. The weather,
though sufficiently cold for
overcoats, is obviously sunny
and pleasant enough to sit in
a steamer chair and quietly
read, smoke or chat, and the
ocean is suspiciously calm and
smooth. The Dominion Line
was one of several companies
operating services to Canada
and was owned partly by
Cunard. It carried
considerable numbers of
emigrants across the Atlantic
at this period but also
publicised its services for
leisure travel.

Artist: William Cossens
Date: June 1904
Registered by: Turner
& Dunnett, Liverpool
PRO reference: COPY 1/217i
folio 31

PLATE 46

Cunard Line

Cunard spans the Atlantic: this poster puts across its message very effectively, with no words except the company's name in enormous lettering. The company flag showing a lion rampant clutching a small globe between his front paws reinforces the idea, and the large globe, standing out beautifully against its dark background, has Cunard's routes picked out in red for extra emphasis. The most important sector of the shipping line's business was the regular passenger and freight service between Liverpool and New York, and at this time the company had seven liners engaged in the North Atlantic trade.

Artist: Paul Hubner
Date: April 1908
Registered by: W E Tucker & Co., London EC
PRO reference: COPY 1/268 folio 23

PLATE 47

Cunard Line

Royal Mail Steamers

This Cunard advertisement is more specifc in terms of information than the previous one, plate 46, but has less immediate impact. It shows the ill-fated *Lusitania*, which later met its end at the hands of a German torpedo-boat in May 1915, leaving Liverpool for the North Atlantic run. When this poster was produced, the *Lusitania* and her sister ship the *Mauretania* were the largest and fastest vessels in the world. The *Lusitania* could carry up to 500 first-class passengers, 500 second-class and 1300 third, with a crew of 800–900. Its lavish accommodation was comparable with that of the palatial hotels of the period.

Artist: Charles Dixon
Date: December 1907
Registered by: Thomas Forman & Sons, Nottingham
PRO reference: COPY 1/264 folio 209

PLATE 48

Pickfords

Winter Sports

These scenes of winter sports on fir-clad snowy hillsides are similar to the Great Northern Railway's winter advertisement (see plate 14). Pickfords travel agency was well established in the Edwardian period and was especially keen to promote winter holidays as a rapidly growing part of the business. Skis were first used for sport in Norway in 1860 and quickly attained popularity elsewhere in Scandinavia and in the Alps. Before this holidays in Switzerland or the French Alps were mostly summer walking or climbing trips. Ski-jumping, pictured on this poster, soon sprang up as a variation. Tobogganning and bobsleighing too suddenly became the smart sports to enjoy, particularly where there were purpose-built runs such as the Cresta Run at St Moritz.

Artist: John Henry Lloyd
Date: November 1911
Registered by: Johnson, Riddle & Co. Ltd
PRO reference: COPY 1/315ii folio 158

PLATE 49

A.1. Tours

Consulting the "Which"

Here we have a poster produced by another enterprising London firm which organised travel in Britain and Europe. In the words of the original copyright registration document, we see a 'witch and cauldron, with tourist at side watching various towns and views appearing in the smoke.' The pun in the heading no doubt appealed to the Edwardian taste for rather laboured verbal witticisms, but in modern times it seems endearingly unsophisticated.

Artist: Arthur Ernest Leggatt
Date: March 1908
Registered by: A.1 Cooperation Shipping and Tourist Society Ltd
PRO reference: COPY 1/267 folio 105

PLATE 50

Midland Railway

Cook's Excursions to London

This poster and the next come from the series produced by David Allen and Sons for the Midland Railway in 1904. Most of them were registered at Stationers' Hall as just the basic image and heading, leaving space for further information to be added later. The same design could thus be used for excursions on different dates, perhaps with different times or prices. It makes a striking advertisement for trips to London, using traditional and easily identifiable images of the capital but in an uncluttered and memorable way.

Artist: Howard Sommerville
Date: October 1904
Registered by: David Allen & Sons
PRO reference: COPY 1/221 folio 261

PLATE 51

Midland Railway

Cook's Excursions to London

This poster is very similar in style to the preceding one, though by a different artist. Again the London symbols – the statue of Eros, the bobby, the flower-girl, ubiquitous in Edwardian London – are juxtaposed effectively. Its strong blues and yellows recall the Carrick-a-Rede poster (plate 36) designed by Dennis Fitzsimmons at the same time. Again space has been left for additional information to be overprinted later, providing details of trips to the city arranged by Thomas Cook and the Midland Railway. The line's headquarters were in Derby and they operated services from virtually all the big cities in the Midlands and the north into their terminus at St Pancras.

Artist: Dennis Fitzsimmons
Date: October 1904
Registered by: David Allen & Sons
PRO reference: COPY 1/221 folio 248

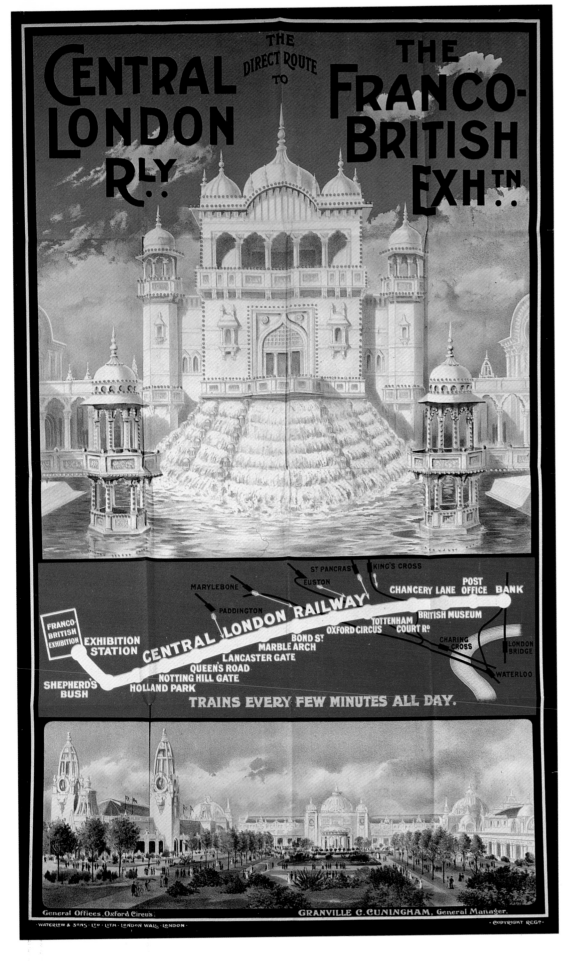

PLATE 52

Central London Railway

The Franco-British Exhibition

After the Great Exhibition of 1851, similar international shows had been held almost every year in cities of Europe and America. In a sense they were a modern equivalent of the great medieval fairs, although the idea was not so much to sell goods directly as to make them known. The Franco-British Exhibition of 1908 was a little more focused – as its name implies, it was held to foster awareness of the produce and manufactured goods of Britain and France. The poster shows part of the impressive White City Hall and water cascade with a general view of the site below. Between them is a map of the Central London Railway, one of the early Tube lines. In 1908 a loop was added at the west end of the line with a new station in Wood Lane specially for the opening of the Franco-British Exhibition. Some of the station names have changed since 1908: Exhibition Station is now White City, Queen's Road is Queensway, British Museum is Holborn and Post Office is now St Paul's.

Artist: William Tomkin
Date: August 1908
Registered by: Waterlow & Sons Ltd
PRO reference: COPY 1/272 folio 216

PLATE 53

Central London (Tube) Railway

Shopping Centres

This elegant, wasp-waisted young woman with her small but perfectly formed parcel is the epitome of the smart, wealthy customer up in town for her Christmas shopping. No hansom cab for her – the convenience of the Tube is exactly what she wants. The Central London Railway was also well aware of the extra custom to be gained from the January sales: in 1911 they issued a five-shilling 'shopping season ticket' for the whole month of January – a bargain, but for female passengers only!

Artist: Edward Sharland
Date: December 1908
Registered by: Waterlow & Sons Ltd
PRO reference: COPY 1/276 folio 121

PLATE 54

Underground

The Only Way to the Theatre

The dark interior of this typically ornate Edwardian theatre, and the curious mixture of slogans at the bottom of the poster, make a sombre background in contrast to the brilliantly lit stage curtain with its important message. Advertisements for the Tube began to use this typeface for the word 'underground' in 1911. By this time much of the Tube, in central London at any rate, had been electrified and was acknowledged to be much cleaner than before. It was therefore more attractive as a means of transport if you were going out for the evening and wanted still to look your best when you arrived at the theatre.

Artist: Frederick Taylor
Date: April 1912
Registered by: Johnson, Riddle & Co. Ltd
PRO reference: COPY 1/320 folio 158

PLATE 55

Central London Railway
The Tube

A most unusual way to promote the underground Central London Railway – the company was certainly making a great effort to persuade passengers of the comfort and convenience of the Tube. In fact a new system of air purification and ventilation for the stations and tunnels had just been installed. Air was brought in from outside, filtered and mixed with a refreshing dose of ozone in a purification chamber, and thence distributed to the system. A heating or cooling coil was placed in the chamber to regulate the air temperature.

Artist: John Henry Lloyd
Date: July 1911
Registered by: Johnson, Riddle & Co. Ltd
PRO reference: COPY 1/310 folio 46

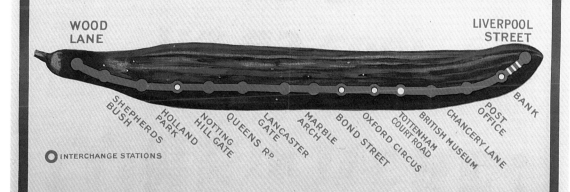

PLATE 56

Central London (Tube) Railway

This is another illustration of the Central London Railway's contention that the Tube was cool and comfortable. Perhaps they were right if London was suffering one of its periodic smogs at ground level. Here we have a wonderful allegorical picture of Father Neptune rising from the waves and delivering a blast of ozone through a glass tube, inside which is a miniature Underground train. This was designed by the same artist as the cucumber poster; he was a master of the quirky and unexpected.

Artist: John Henry Lloyd
Date: October 1911
Registered by: Johnson, Riddle & Co. Ltd
PRO reference: COPY 1/314 folio 234

PLATE 57

Underground

Golder's Green

The noxious, polluted air of the city, thickened by the smoke from countless chimneys, gives way to a soft, undulating landscape of heath and lake – was Golders Green ever thus? Or was the artist trapped in his urban inferno and simply imagining a sunlit rural paradise floating serenely above him? A series of posters was published at this time exhorting passengers to venture forth and enjoy the delights of London's suburban fringes. It was all part of the new vogue for health and fitness seized on by canny railway advertising departments and used in much of their publicity.

Artist: one or more of James McClery, Hampden Butler, Sydney Briault and Alfred Glossop (artists who shared a studio and took common responsibility for any commercial design work)
Date: January 1911
Registered by: Delittle, Fenwick & Co., York
PRO reference: COPY 1/302 folio 34

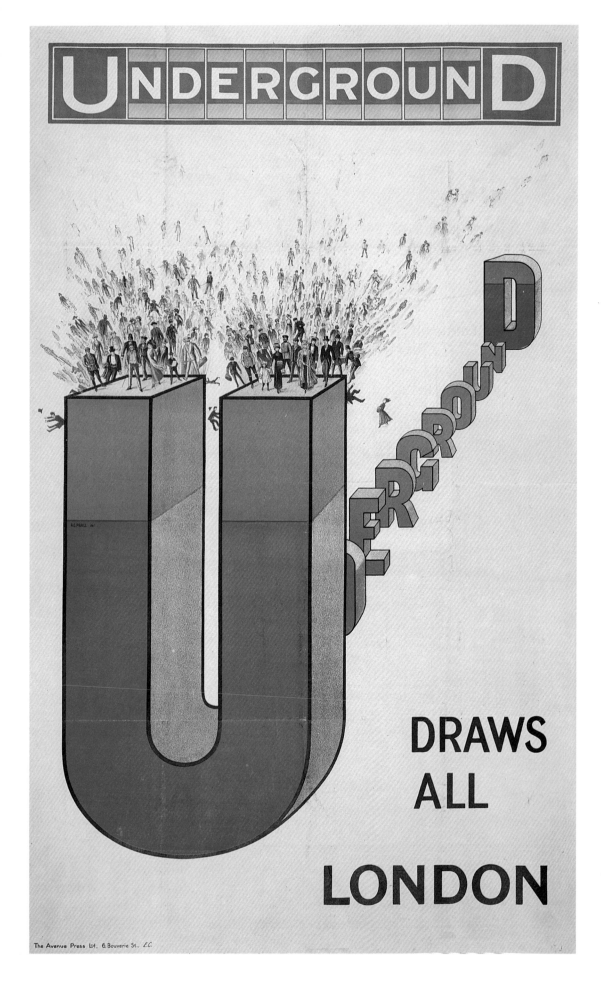

PLATE 58

Underground

Draws All London

A neat conceit: the immense magnet forms the initial letter of Underground and inexorably draws the tiny people of London into the Tube system, with no more will than if they had been iron filings. This is another example, like plate 54, of general Underground promotion using the new typeface which was to prove so enduring. As soon as arrangements were made for tickets issued by any individual line to be usable throughout the system, Londoners and tourists alike very quickly came to regard the Tube as the most convenient form of travel in the capital.

Artist: Reginald George Praill
Date: January 1911
Registered by: The Avenue Press Ltd
PRO reference: COPY 1/302 folio 20

PLATE 59

Central London (Tube) Railway

Lightning Parcel Express

A delightful picture of Oxford Circus with youths on delivery tricycles rushing away in all directions with parcels. The *Railway and Travel Monthly* wrote approvingly of the new service in October 1911: 'the Central London Railway has already decided to collect, as well as deliver, the parcels, and employs for this purpose a number of tricycle carriers, which are decorated with the words "Central London Railway (Tube) Lightning Parcels Express". Seeing that the parcels are hauled by "harnessed lightning", the adjective, which well typifies the speed with which parcels are conveyed, is not inappropriate. Many packages have been conveyed from the City to the West End and delivered to the consignees in well under 40 minutes.'

Artist: John Henry Lloyd
Date: November 1911
Registered by: Johnson, Riddle & Co. Ltd
PRO reference: COPY 1/315i folio 63

LONDON & NORTH WESTERN RAILWAY

EUSTON

**BEST NIGHT TRAINS TO
LIVERPOOL, MANCHESTER, SCOTLAND & IRELAND.**

FREDERICK HARRISON, GENERAL MANAGER.

PLATE 60

London & North Western Railway

Euston

Chicago in the 1930s? No, London in 1905. The strong contrast between the dark blues and bright golden yellow makes this spirited poster hum with life. A great sense of energy and urgency spills out from it as the cabs jostle through the immense arch, dramatically silhouetted against the darkening evening sky sprinkled with stars. The London and North Western Railway's Euston terminus is portrayed as the gateway to the glorious and unknown, from which any lucky passengers catching a night train to travel north are not simply making a journey; they are on the eve of adventure.

Artist: Douglas George Brown
Date: May 1905
Registered by: McCorquodale & Co. Ltd
PRO reference: COPY 1/229ii folio 204